P9-DNY-735

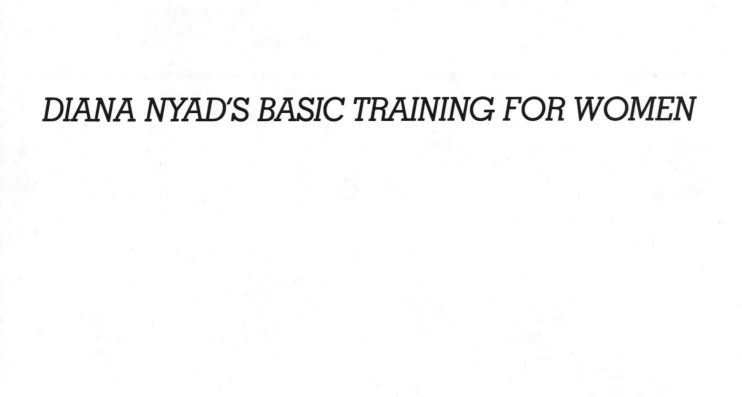

DIANA NYAD'S BASIC TRAINING FOR WOMEN

DIANA NYAD'S
Basic Training

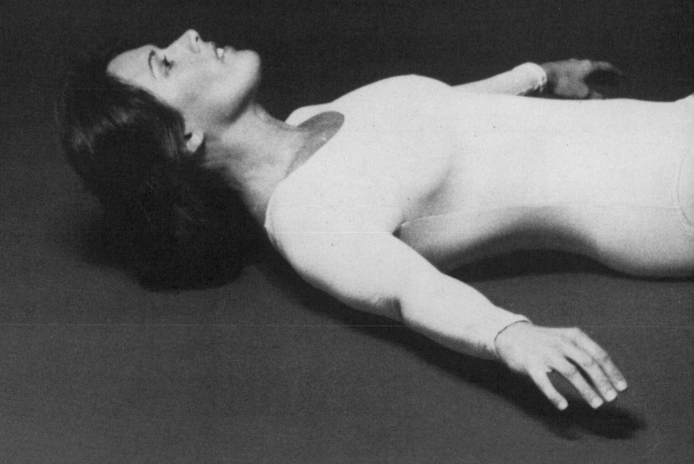

for Women

Diana Nyad and
Candace Lyle Hogan

H

Harmony Books / New York

Designed by Constance T. Doyle
Photographs by Michael Ian

Copyright © 1981 by Diana Nyad, Candace Lyle
Hogan and Hilltown Press, Inc.

All rights reserved. No part of this book may be re-
produced or utilized in any form or by any means,
electronic or mechanical, including photocopying,
recording, or by any information storage and re-
trieval system, without permission in writing from
the publisher.

Inquiries should be addressed to Harmony Books,
a division of Crown Publishers, Inc., One Park
Avenue, New York, New York 10016

Printed in the United States of America

Published simultaneously in Canada by General
Publishing Company Limited

Library of Congress Cataloging in Publication Data

Nyad, Diana.
    Diana Nyad's Basic training for women.

    1. Exercise for women.   2. Physical fitness.
I. Hogan, Candace Lyle.   II. Title.   III. Title:
Basic training for women.
GV482.N9   1981   613.7'045   81-4256
                                        AACR2

ISBN: 0-517-544555

10 9 8 7 6 5 4 3 2 1
First Edition

*To the family of women—our own, our mothers'
and our daughters' generations . . .*

CONTENTS

ACKNOWLEDGMENTS

It's been an enriching two years spent in collaboration with my coauthor Candace Lyle Hogan. Neither of us could have produced alone a thorough guide so specifically appropriate to you. Thanks to literary agent Liz Darhansoff for her professional persistence in keeping the project alive over the long term so that it had a chance to thrive under the enthusiasm of Harmony Books editor Harriet Bell; and three cheers to both of them for beginning Basic Training on their own and enjoying it. Special thanks to Susan Bolotin for being the kind of editor anyone could trust. Thanks to Dr. Marigold Edwards of the University of Pittsburgh for being such a stickler for fact. And thanks to the Paris Health Club of New York City, my training grounds, for bending over backward in allowing us to take over during photography sessions for the book.

INTRODUCTION

I want you to think of me as your coach. This book, my locker room speech to you, is called *Basic Training for Women* and you are reading it because you want to make your body stronger and enrich the quality of your life. Like every good coach's locker room speech, it is meant to inspire you and give you confidence and to arm you with every instructional detail you'll need before going out there on your own. If you read and follow *Basic Training* with the same thoroughness and care that I applied to the researching and writing of it, you will understand the pleasure and satisfaction that I have felt as a professional athlete. You will experience that same pleasure and satisfaction yourself.

It doesn't matter that you're not a professional athlete. It's all right if you're unfamiliar with athletic attitudes, jargon or sensations. Don't fret if you're moderately overweight or unhappy with the tone of your thigh, hip or stomach muscles. You just need Basic Training—not a crash program that fanatically precludes other priorities in your life but rather a thirty-minute-a-day lifetime *process* through which you can reach and maintain your ideal weight, as well as gain solid, firm muscle tone. Basic Training introduces you to the athletic world through precise, reassuring, step-by-step instructions.

If you've been working out, in one way or another, for more than a year now and feel reasonably satisfied with your weight, your muscle tone and your athletic prowess, you still need Basic Training. It offers you the subtleties of physical technique and mental training that twenty-two years of experience and a lifetime of good athletic instincts have taught me.

You may be extremely active with your career or your family—or both—and fear that any strenuous exercises would push you over the edge to collapse. Or you may think you're too old to start exercising for the first time in thirty years—or for the first time ever. Stop worrying! Vigorous, strenuous, regular activity—like sport, like play—is mentally and physically exhilarating. Basic Training will refresh you, restore your energy, and drive the mental and physical stress out of your system; it is something to look forward to every day. It will enable you to go for many more hours before feeling aches or pains or fatigue because you will be strengthening your legs, stomach, back, all of your skeletal muscles as well as your heart and lungs. You will be able to stand, walk, sit, run up steps or chase little ones all day with plenty of energy to spare. Basic Training will give you a mental, as well as a physical, high because it stimulates all your physiological systems to a peak. I have a friend who works a frenzied, high-stress fifteen-hour day for network television. She used to get to the office at 6:00 A.M., break for a heavy lunch in the middle of the day and then struggle under the weight of lazy fatigue until about 9:00 P.M. Now she skips the heavy lunch, goes to her health club for Basic Training and grabs a juice and a yogurt on her way back to the office. Her workout makes her "high" and carries her through the rest of the day. My sister experiences the same renewed energy from Basic Training, although her stress comes from a long day with a two-and-a-half-year-old and an infant. By their bedtime she is ready to collapse but instead she gets out for a run—while her husband keeps an eye on the kids—and comes back relaxed and "up."

I travel all over the country—big cities, small

towns—talking with women of all ages, all economic backgrounds, all physical histories and lifestyles. If you are like any of these women I have met, I am the right coach for you. I understand your situation, and I believe in your potential. Sportswriter Candace Lyle Hogan and I have thoroughly researched your special physiology as a woman, as well as the particular sociological hurdles that face all women. I know what is realistic to ask of you, in terms of time and in terms of ability.

We Americans, both female and male, do not generally take care of our bodies through regular exercise and decent nutrition. Strength and physical prowess have little earning power in our technological society, and we are too lazy or apathetic or uneducated about health and fitness to make recreational, *strenuous* exercise a part of our daily lives. Consequently, obesity and coronary heart disease in our country have grown to epidemic proportions. The new statistics about millions of joggers and racquetball players are encouraging but insignificant compared with the numbers of inactive overeaters and overdrinkers.

But women, more than men, need Basic Training, and you can benefit from it more dramatically. You have a higher percentage of body fat than men. (And sex discrimination may have given you a negative feeling about physical expression or shortchanged you by denying you any sports background at all.) In a word, you need a good coach. I want you to look better—more muscle, less fat, firmer thighs and buttocks and breasts, clearer eyes, better skin tone. I want you to feel better—to have a higher energy level all day long, luscious deep sleeps, more flexibility when you wake up in the morning, better sex, sensual enjoyment of the right foods, easier menstrual periods, easier pregnancies. I want you to develop a stable basis for self-esteem, self-worth, self-respect. I want you to be proud and secure about everything you do and every way that you are. I want you on my team.

I am a good coach and I have taken very delicate care in preparing Basic Training. It's true that I have been paid for my time, but more motivates my efforts than that. I am deeply excited that women are truly on the brink of breaking the chains of social tyranny. Women, individually, are about to discover their potential as men have for centuries before them. This potential is intellectual and emotional and economic and social; I believe, however, that physical strength and courage is at the very root of self-respect and self-worth in all endeavors.

I look forward to working with you, but I must warn you that I'm tough. I need your commitment and I'll expect this commitment on two counts. First, that you follow Basic Training the way it is taught, to the letter. Second, that you understand it to be a *lifetime* involvement. Basic Training is to help you achieve optimum mental and physical health for the rest of your life—not just to achieve quick temporary weight loss. Don't question me if you do only half the workouts; don't complain if you dedicate yourself to my program for a year, but then get out of the daily habit during Christmas vacation. I can be your coach IF AND ONLY IF you commit yourself as a Basic Training athlete; only if you will make this commitment to yourself.

I ask for only 30 minutes a day. Thirty regular, intense minutes that will strengthen your body and enhance your life. Read the book from cover to cover before beginning. Remember, it's my locker room speech to you. The Basic Training workouts alone are meaningless without the knowledge of why you are undertaking the program. Part I is full of background ammunition on your psyche, your heart, and your muscles—how your body works. In Part II I show you how to dig in with the desire and the perseverance of a world champion, even though you will be putting in an average of only 30 minutes a day. In the Weight-Training Manual (Part III) there are instructions and photographs to show you exactly how to perform resistance exercises with free weights and Universal and Nautilus machines for maximum benefit of muscle tone and strength, as demanded in Basic Training participation. And, after working with you for a few months, if you discover that you are a more experienced athlete than I guessed, you will move out of Basic Training and on to the more challenging workouts outlined in the Advanced Training Manual (also in Part III). I will also teach you the tricky nuances of various situations you might encounter as an athlete (Inside Tips); explain how to use health club facilities (The

Sport and Health Club Primer); and outline some fundamentals of nutrition (The Diet Primer) all in Part IV. Please consult a sports-oriented physician before beginning Basic Training if you feel you are too overweight, if you are over thirty years old, if you have heart or other medical problems or if you have not exercised for several years.

Basic Training is not a bag of tricks and it's not based on faddish concepts. It will take methodical participation before you understand automatically, by experience, everything you will read in this book in a few hours. But, eventually, you will no sooner let a day go by without performing Basic Training than you would let a day go by without brushing your teeth. To make this team you must believe you can do anything, even if you must build yourself up gradually. Never say "I can't." You can. I will show you how.

DIANA NYAD'S BASIC TRAINING FOR WOMEN

PART I
PRE-TRAINING CONDITIONING

CHAPTER 1

The Mind

I am a professional athlete. I started a rigorous training program at the age of ten and I have been using my body as the instrument of my sport, swimming, for twenty-two years. As a result, I know my body just as a concert violinist knows her violin. I am familiar with its many subtleties—I know the capability of my muscles and know how to differentiate between healthy soreness and the warning signs of injury. I also know mental tricks that help me bounce back from failure, keep motivation at a peak and overcome fatigue and boredom.

I assume that you are not a professional athlete. You may participate in one or two sports and do some light exercise, but when it comes to training your body seriously, you are probably a novice. This book is your introduction to physical conditioning and is designed to help you master your instrument. But before we get right down to physical conditioning—the heart and the muscles, why and how you should cultivate them—you could probably use some tips on psychological, emotional and social conditioning.

Like many women, you may be a tiger in lamb's clothing, holding your body in check, denying yourself physical exertion for a variety of reasons. You were probably taught from an early age that developed muscles and profuse sweating are exclusively aspects of the male domain. They are not—they are essential aspects of the *human* domain. No animal, male or female, can be optimally healthy if restricted from movement. A tiger suffers both physically and emotionally when caged. And we humans are no different—regular exercise promotes not only better physical health but better mental health as well.

If you are reading this book, you have made the decision to cultivate your body—for a longer life, for day-to-day physical well-being and renewed energy, for a more attractive appearance, for greater self-confidence and for sheer enjoyment. If you don't yet know your abilities or limitations, don't worry. I am here to coach you. I will gradually introduce you to the wonders of training. Forget why you have never before committed yourself to regular strenuous activity. Regardless of your age, emotional or physical conditioning, begin Basic Training as soon as you have finished reading this book. Pick a day—tomorrow or three or four days from now—and stick to it. The exhilaration that comes from physical exertion will be enough to maintain your momentum once you get started.

But getting started may not be easy. Your muscles will ache, or you might worry about suffering an injury. Unlike a sociable game of tennis, a training session involves you and you alone. You may have no one to encourage you, to share your stress and strain. At times you'll wonder whether you're pushing yourself too hard, and you'll have to call on your own inner resources to see you through. When you begin, you will be both inspired and confused by unfamiliar sensations.

What It Feels Like to Start

It's important to start out right. Beginning the wrong way gives you an easy excuse to quit entirely. The most common excuses are minor pains and the fear of injury.

Ninety-nine percent of the time, you can avoid

injury by attending to basic procedures of prevention. Always warm up your muscles and ligaments with the stretching exercises, which I'll detail later. As you become more physically active, you will begin to know your body, know it well enough to sense when something is going awry, when just a bit more stress or fatigue will result in damage. The thing to do then is to stop and rest. Contrary to the popular mythology of football, there is no valor and not much glory in pushing yourself beyond reason.

However. You *do* need to push yourself some. Each day your Basic Training will challenge you with a beginning, a middle and an end. You may need to force yourself to begin and to push yourself to stick with it to the finish. There's only one valid reason to stop before the completion of your daily routine. And that reason, not likely to happen to you, is injury. Take my word for it, you'll know if you are injured. Bad pain would tell you so and you'd heed its message. But do not—and this is very important—do not mistake normal discomfort for bad pain. As your coach, I don't want you to quit; I want you to thrive through discovery. In order to achieve benefit from this kind of exploration and experience, you have to go the distance.

When you begin Basic Training, you'll enter a world of physical sensations (and even emotional feelings) of great variety and intensity. The type and gradations of these sensations will be new to many of you. The unknown is fraught with fear but not necessarily with danger. I can assure you that valuable experience lies on the other side of that fear. You can overcome fear; I'll show you how.

Some of the new sensations you're going to experience will feel suspiciously like pain. I want you to experiment with this kind of sensation right now so that you begin to get rid of the fear of it, so that you'll know what I mean when I say intensity, what it feels like to put your muscles to work for you. Begin learning the difference between "good pain" and "bad pain." This is what the following experiment is for. Demonstrate for yourself the difference between good pain or harmless discomfort and bad pain, which is your signal to stop.

Put on comfortably loose shorts or sweat pants and rubber-soled shoes, which won't slip on the floor. Make sure you have a clock or a watch with a second hand in view. Stand with your back to a wall or some firm straight-backed surface such as a door, placing your heels about 12 inches apart and about 16 inches from the wall.

Put your hand behind you to balance yourself against the wall and bend your knees as if you're beginning to sit down in an imaginary chair. When you have bent your knees enough so that your thighs are level with your knees and parallel to the floor, lean your back and buttocks against the wall and remove your hand. This is the position of 90/90's—two 90 second periods at a 90-degree angle—the exercise that will introduce you to good pain.

This is how you should look: feet placed flat on the floor making your lower legs perpendicular to the floor so that they form 90-degree angles with your thighs at the knees; toes pointed straight ahead of you; feet about 12 inches apart; arms hanging loosely at your sides. Don't use your arms or hands in any way to support your weight. (Check the photograph on page 78 for form.)

The wall is your chair back; you look as if you are sitting in a chair but you have no chair. Now *try* to hold that position for 90 seconds—a terrific way to test your willpower.

This stationary exercise begins as soon as you've removed your supporting hand from the wall and are relying upon your quadriceps (the muscles along the tops of the thighs) to support your weight. Begin timing yourself. Remember: The goal is 90 seconds at one stretch. You probably won't be able to do it the first time out, but really try. Here is how you're going to feel at one time or another during this 90-second period.

Right away, after only about 10 seconds have passed, you're starting to feel a warm sensation in your thighs. You notice how the long muscle at the top of each thigh is flexed, feeling firm to the touch. Breathe—rhythmically, calmly.

As the seconds tick by, you're passing through different phases of one single sensation. It may feel like dozens of various sensations, but in fact what you are feeling is the quadriceps resisting gravity. When you are standing up, your skeleton more than your muscles is supporting your weight. But when you are bent like this in 90/90's, your position

How to Get Started

After you have begun exercising each day, momentum (and a few tricks, see p. 30) will help you complete the routine despite occasional boredom. But what gets you started each day? Basic Training restores your energy to you, but how do you marshal the will for Basic Training if your energy is low after a long day's work?

If you're having trouble getting motivated on a particular day, take the following steps. Do them one by one, ritualistically. Even though your heart might not be in it, taking specific action will help you to break the spell of inertia.

1. Put on your exercise clothes if you do Basic Training at home, or pack up your gear if you're going to the gym, health club or Y.

2. Focus on your goals: Would you like to wear a certain style of slacks that you never thought you could fit into? Would you like to receive any of the benefits you see listed on p. 65? Would you like to feel more energetic and intense than you're feeling right now? Focus on the fact that this upcoming workout will bring you closer to your goal.

3. Although you're a beginner, try to think of yourself as an old hand like me. You've just come home from work and you have a choice—you can either loll around or you can do your workout. What would motivate me in that situation? Well, I would remind myself that I've felt more fatigued, and slightly depressed, on the days I've done no workouts, whereas I've felt great every time after I've exercised. If the workout went well, I felt exhilarated; if it had been rough, it felt great to know that it was over. But if lolling around suddenly appeals to you instead of a workout, think of how much more you'll enjoy lolling around *after* your workout.

4. Focus on the idea that you're going to make your whole day better by making Basic Training a part of it. Even the things that happened earlier in the day will seem less upsetting because of it.

5. Call a friend, if you need more inspiration, and ask her or him to meet you at the gym or come over to do your workout with you.

6. If you still feel lazy after performing all these rituals, bribe yourself. Promise yourself a treat as a reward for doing your workout today, and then get to it.

Fitness training, like sport, is essentially play, a pleasure and an enjoyment that keeps you going back for more. Even while I am in training for a long swim, swimming 8 hours a day for months at a time, I still find myself popping into the ocean once in a while simply for some horseplay. Swimming is my work, but it is also my pleasure. Whatever it takes for you to get yourself started, it's going to be worth it.

Yet there will be some days when you just don't feel like doing your workout. If you *really* don't want to, don't—or turn to p. 169 and learn how to cheat on Basic Training. You'll find that after taking a day off, perhaps even two, you'll begin to miss your routine and hunger for the activity again. But there will be times when you'll need to discipline yourself out of slumps. On days that you are not very eager, try going through the motions anyway. Perhaps your energy will be rekindled once you get a little sweat going. Sometimes just lacing up your sneakers makes the heart beat faster. You'll discover that, yes, you really would like to train today. Also there are ways (see p. 24) to incorporate Basic Training into your life that will render you less susceptible to slumps and more successful at maintaining the regularity of your workouts.

---

of resistance against gravity is far different. This position calls upon your quadriceps (and to a lesser degree the muscles of the back of the thigh, the buttocks and the calves) to prevent you from slipping down to the floor with the pull of gravity. To do this work the quadriceps are in an isometric (stationary) contraction, a position that never hurt Charles Atlas, and is not going to hurt you.

So don't be afraid; or, rather, if you are afraid, don't give in to the fear. And don't anticipate what you're going to feel next. For one thing, you simply don't know what you're going to feel next unless you persevere long enough to find out. Furthermore, the discomfort of this type of exercise does not necessarily increase in a linear way—it comes, it goes; it subsides and changes. Everyone is different, but, for example, you may feel a seemingly unbearable burning after only 15 seconds in this position. But what makes it feel "unbearable"? Not because it actually is, but because you're afraid if you do endure it, maybe something bad will happen to you, something will click, snap or explode. No way. Nothing's going to happen to you. In fact, even if you feel what you would call pain after only 15 seconds, if you keep your position, that feeling will subside for a while. You're getting used to it; you're thinking about something else now—reciting a poem, humming a tune—taking your mind off your fear.

That will take you to at least 30 seconds. Then maybe another crisis moment. Thirty or 60 seconds have passed—you feel as if you can't go on. The burning licks hotter and hotter. Your legs are quivering. You're starting to grimace. Your eyes are in a squint. Your teeth are clenching. Calm down; relax your face—grimacing wastes energy. You're breathing more rapidly now. You're beginning to worry. The feeling in your thighs is fiery—it seems like pain, but it is merely intensity. Pain is what tells you to stop; but this feeling is warm and diffuse, not sharp and focused like real or bad pain would be, so you don't stop. You try to stick with it because muscles thrive on intensity.

Seventy-five seconds have passed. Your buttocks are beginning to slip down the wall. Your feet are losing their exact positioning on the floor. There's a forest fire raging along the tops of your thighs; the beads of sweat on your forehead are not enough to put it out. But you have only 15 seconds left! You can last 15 seconds! Stay with it! This is your coach talking now: 15 seconds . . . 10 seconds . . . only 5 seconds more . . . tick, tick . . . 90! Get up.

Using your hand against the wall for support, you rise slowly from the imaginary chair and walk around the room, shaking your legs out loosely, gently, but proudly. Your legs still feel warm, but now with a kind of pleasurable tingle. You can strut now, and well you should. That wasn't so bad, was

it? Well, even if it was, it's over, right? And not only has nothing bad come of it, but something good has come of it: Because you did it this time, next time it will be easier to do and if you didn't hold the position for the full 90 seconds, next time you'll hold it longer. The discomfort may have seemed painful to you, but it wasn't bad pain, because it was not signaling to you danger of injury. Rather, the muscles were signaling to you: We're working, we'll keep you up, we can do what you ask of us; if you can do it, so can we. That's good pain's message. Try to hear it throughout Basic Training.

Depending upon your condition, you may not have been able to do the 90 seconds continuously on your first try. In fact, you probably weren't able to. But you will someday. You can work up to the full continuous 90 seconds. And, in the chapter outlining Basic Training, I'll tell you exactly how to complete the two required 90/90's everyday. But right now, you're simply acquainting yourself with the stages of good pain.

The number of seconds it will take before the legs quiver with fatigue will vary for each person. The point is, become familiar with your own state of conditioning and how the process of improving it will feel to you. There is some mystery in this, but definitely no danger. These are the natural processes of intensity, and although they may feel strange and unfamiliar to you now, they need not be truly painful or even unpleasant. In the gradations of sensations you will experience in Basic Training, even in the grueling 90/90's, there will be many elements of pleasure. Did you touch your thigh during the exercise? It felt warm, especially the long sinewy part of the thigh which was showing itself in a more defined manner than usual. It felt warm because it was warm under the skin too. All muscle exertion creates heat and it was that heat under the skin that licked and burned during your 90/90's.

Now that you know how muscle intensity feels, let's preview what it feels like to use those muscles to give your heart and lungs an intense workout. Let's take a look at what may happen your first day out. Imagine that you've decided to run, without stopping, a distance of one mile, in ten minutes, after determining that at your age, in your condition, you can handle this distance at this pace on your first day.

Early on, everything is pleasant. How invigorating this is—how interesting the landscape, how good the air feels against your face. Sweat begins to bead on your skin. You curl your tongue above your upper lip and taste the salt.

Then, a bit suddenly, it hits you. This is not exactly what marathoners call "hitting the wall" but it may as well be. You're not 18 miles into a 26-mile run, but you're not 10 minutes into a hot tub, either. You're short of breath. The taking of oxygen seems to require an upheaval of your shoulders and entire chest to pump air in and out of your lungs. Your throat is dry because now your mouth is doing what your nose is accustomed to doing. You had assumed your heart was lodged firmly in your chest, somewhat slightly beneath the left breast, but now it seems lodged in your neck, thumping. Constriction in the chest, sandpaper in the throat, perhaps even a stitch in your side, indeed it occurs to you that this sort of activity might be postponed until some later date!

You are just about to suggest this to your body, an adversary at the moment, when you realize your body is really doing just fine. Hmmm. You begin to breathe through your nose and out through the mouth, from the diaphragm, not the upper chest. As you keep running, you reach the point of a new understanding. You've discovered what's called a second wind and there might just be a third or fourth as well. You keep an even pace, breathe rhythmically and don't panic. You are going to see this thing through.

Until now, your muscles seemed to be outlasting your heart and lungs. But you notice a strange reversal. Slowly at first, then with greater force, a funny sensation begins to creep up your thigh. This hurts. Pain is supposed to be the body's warning signal, the prelude to danger. But this pain doesn't feel like a serious warning; it is less localized, not jabbing. This is warm, diffuse pain. It is not enough to stop your run.

You are starting to recognize the difference between good pain and bad pain during aerobic activity. At the end of your prescribed distance, you realize that your mind and your body have helped

each other out, each preventing the other from quitting.

The first run is over and you feel a sense of accomplishment, the memory of which will become a motivating force the next time. Immediately after strenuous activity, you might feel weak and light-headed, reactions you can avoid by not stopping cold. Cool down by walking and stretching. The dizziness you may feel after you stop short is due to the sudden reduction of blood flow to the brain. During the run your heart was working hard to pump blood into your extremities; in turn your muscles were working to send blood back to the heart. When you stop exercising suddenly, the heart continues pumping fast for a time, but the natural force of contracting muscles has stopped sending the blood back forcefully for recycling. A gradual reduction in activity after vigorous exertion will give your body the chance to reorient its processes and bring them in line with a less strenuous mode of activity such as walking.

To minimize the soreness that comes from initial strength building, and to keep from tightening up after your workout, devote a few minutes to this "cool down" process, just as you will with the warm-up exercises. Soreness, stiffness in muscles, tendons, ligaments and joints, are all aspects of the good pain that comes from changing an inert life to an active one. Muscles ache, often more so a day or two after exercise than during the following two hours, because of a buildup of lactic acid, a waste product. Lactic acid accumulates in muscles when the circulatory system fails to provide the muscles with adequate nourishment during exercise. After cooling off, a massage, hot tub, whirlpool bath or just a long, hot shower will increase the circulation and that helps dispel the lactic acid buildup. These periods of soreness will decrease in length and severity the more regularly active you are.

What Has Taken You So Long?

My upbringing was, I suppose, unusual in the encouragement and the independence I experienced as a girl growing up in the fifties and sixties. Beginning at the age of ten, I got up before 5:00 A.M. 365

How to Keep Going on a Daily Basis

1. Schedule your workout for a certain period of time each day that will be the most convenient for you. Stick with that time. If you find that changes in your life-style make another time of day more convenient, then change your schedule. It doesn't matter physiologically when you do your workouts—that's individual choice. What does matter is that you make a schedule in advance and that you stick to it. Making your Basic Training workouts a priority in your life is necessary if you are to achieve the essential consistency of effort.

2. If you wish, start Basic Training with a friend and schedule your sessions together. On the days when your own motivation is low, the simple prospect of a partner waiting for you at the appointed hour at the gym will prod you along. You can't depend upon someone else to make you be on time and regular with your workouts, but you can rely on a friend for some commiseration and encouragement, and even a little

competition and peer pressure, if that helps. Choose your Basic Training companion wisely: She should be as committed as you are to concentrating on the workouts and to saving the socializing for afterward.

3. Coordinate other commitments with the timing and place of your workouts. On certain days of the week, make an appointment to meet a friend somewhere close by the gym for a time shortly after finishing your workout. That will give you added incentive to do your workout and to get there on time.

4. Keep your exercise clothes together in a special drawer. If possible, stock up on extra sets of shorts, T-shirts and socks so that dirty laundry can never provide you with an easy excuse to postpone Basic Training.

5. Keep a log of your workouts. In a pocket-size notebook or on a calendar, write in your workout schedule in advance for the month, and then mark daily what you did during the workout, how

long it took you, and, if you like, how you felt about it. If you didn't do it, write in why not. Like the attainment of any goal of value, becoming a Basic Training athlete requires a long-term commitment of time, energy and intelligence. Charting your course in advance and monitoring it every day will let you learn from your mistakes and to adjust your scheduling methods over time. For many women, the actual physical workouts themselves will be easier than maintaining the regular scheduling of them. This is not because 30 minutes is a long period of time in a day, but because fitting in any new activity regularly within your present schedule involves some major change in life-style. Attaining an easy, regular rhythm will take time—perhaps six months—so don't be discouraged if your commitment seems erratic at first. Just keep striving for more and more frequency and ultimately you will achieve the regularity of workouts, which is so important.

days a year, Christmas included, for swimming practice. When I turned twelve, my mother gave me a key to the house so I could come and go as my athletic obsession required. Yet I remember that while teachers and peers admired my dedication, they definitely considered my pursuit of the physical a boyish trait.

Today athleticism is not considered boyish. But until the early seventies, the social conditioning of the American female not only limited her athletic opportunities, but also made physical conditioning seem unattainable to her. Until the seventies, our society's working assumption was that the differ-

ences between females and males were so great as to constitute a biological mandate against men cooking and women competing. Of course, we know that rationalization is hogwash—biological differences never justified such rigid behavioral rules. The true villain was, and still is, sex discrimination.

Although sex bias has diminished somewhat, blatant discrimination still exists both in the attitude toward and treatment of women by our society (and that is why we must remain vigilant in our promotion of equal rights). Watch out for the effect that past and present sex discrimination is having on you in your approach to physical exercise. It may be causing you to feel an unreasonable fear of movement or an unrealistic bravado. It may cause you to expect either too little or too much of yourself physically: too little because of myths that say that females are incapable physically; too much because the dashing of those myths might compel you to feel you have to "prove yourself."

Just remember that, as a human being, you are built to move vigorously; and that as an individual you are just as capable of vigorous movement as most men and most women. It is important to stress what most scientists stress—that behavioral differences are due much more to socialization than to gender. Females and males are inherently more similar than they are different; the broadest variation in physical abilities appears *within* each sex, not between the sexes. Experience and practice are a lot more important than gender in the success of physical performance. It stands to reason that any child who climbs trees, falls and gets up again, is more likely to perceive better visually the spatial and geometric features of objects and her own relation to them. So if you never climbed trees as a child, for example, you're going to find Basic Training a more foreign experience than will someone who grew up climbing trees. Your possible initial awkwardness will not be because you're female, but because of the lack of a certain kind of physical practice in your individual background. More women than men lack that kind of background not because females have not been interested in or capable of sports, but because females have been discouraged and barred from participation.

How to Begin

Begin on the day you promised yourself you would. There is a story told about an overweight woman who said, when it came her turn to tell her self-help group what it was she most wanted to do in the world: "I want to be a singer—but I'm waiting until I lose weight before I start my singing career."

"How long have you been overweight?" the group leader asked.

"Ten years," she answered.

"This may seem harsh to hear," said the group leader, "but you're going to be a fat singer. Someday you may lose weight, if that's what you want to do, but right now it's important to start singing. And to begin now, you're going to have to sing fat."

It may be equally tempting to wait until all systems are go before you begin Basic Training—to wait until your daughter is through with her own soccer season, or until the workload of your job lightens up or until after your vacation when you'll have a tan on your legs. Take it from me: Circumstances will never be perfect. Pick a day and stick to it.

On this day you'll find you've got your sneakers on. It isn't important what brand they are or how much they cost. The important thing is that they *fit*—snug around the heel so they don't rub and give you blisters, loose and long enough in the front so they don't cramp your toes. Your shorts or sweat pants and your top should also be comfortable and roomy.

That's all the preparation you need—this book and comfortable clothes. Reading the book and gathering the clothes are the only passive parts of Basic Training. All the rest you will do through action; all the rest you will learn by doing.

Action and Risk

Fortunately, our culture has changed enough so that a woman or girl no longer risks loss of social approval by involving herself in sports or fitness training. But until quite recently the underlying rule of most young girls' "basic training" said: "Avoid all activities involving even a remote risk of pain or injury." These young girls, grown-ups now, are savvy enough to realize that being physical no longer entails the risk of social disapproval. However, subconsciously, exertion may still be enshrouded with contingencies of high risk—risk of failure and injury—and myths that stop many women from taking advantage of their new opportunities. The mystique of the mind that keeps many women away *from* action can only be demystified *through* action.

And here we come to a crucial point about

What You Can Expect over Time if You Train Daily

The following projections of changes you can expect to feel will vary in time and degree depending upon your physical condition when you begin Basic Training. They will also depend upon the intensity and regularity of your commitment. For example, if you are desperately out of shape, you will feel and see changes in the mirror more quickly and dramatically than someone starting out in a better state of fitness. My editor began Basic Training right after she read the first draft of this book. Barely three months later, she had lost twenty-four pounds; she went home for a visit and her mother didn't recognize her.

After one week: You will begin to feel muscles you never felt before. You'll feel soreness. You'll begin to fall asleep quickly and sleep deeply, a sign that you're on the road to shaping up.

After one month: You'll begin to feel the transition, to notice actual physiological changes, such as easier breathing. You'll notice that your muscles are definitely getting stronger and such tasks as climbing stairs with a sack of groceries will be easier than before.

After three months: You'll notice that you've begun to change size somewhat—your thighs are smaller in circumference, firmer, and harder; your stomach and torso are becoming taut, firm, stronger; your chest (supported by more developed pectoral muscles) will be higher; your shoulders, arms and breasts will seem to fill out a blouse differently than before. You'll notice that, with increased grip strength, you'll be opening jars with your hands which you used to have to loosen by a tap on the floor.

After six months: All these changes and more will have occurred; the major transition is complete and will become permanent and even better as long as you maintain Basic Training on a daily basis. Even standing and sitting for long hours will be easy and painless mainly because of the increased muscular endurance in your back. Just as the heart is the key to cardiovascular endurance (signaled by a low resting pulse), the back (the muscles surrounding the spine) is the key to muscular endurance. The abdominals (stomach muscles) are often called the second spine. Much of the effort for all other movements comes from the musculatures of your back and stomach even when those muscles are not directly involved in the movements. If you had to choose only two muscle groups to strengthen, you would choose the back and stomach, but of course you don't have to choose only two. After six months of Basic Training, you will have strengthened all your muscle groups and you will realize it because your strong back and stomach are providing you the firm foundation for all movement, painlessly and injury-free.

Beyond six months: After the first major plateau of transition at six months, you will become a true adventurer—exploring your individual physical potential—and a committed Basic Training athlete whose minimum responsibility is to maintain the cardiovascular and muscular conditioning you have achieved so far and to increase it into your individual peak of fitness. Endurance does not have to decline with age—you may not reach the prime of your endurance until your late forties (see p. 168, Age). But what happens if you slip up, become erratic in your workouts or quit entirely for a time? When you come back to Basic Training after a layoff, it won't take you as long to achieve the strength, the firmness you attained in the first six months. But the degree of cardiovascular fitness you attained in that first six months may take you just as long to regain, since conditioning of the heart and lungs is lost much more quickly than muscular fitness. For example, 15 minutes on a stationary bike after a month off would feel just as difficult as your very first 15 minutes on that bike; whereas your first return to a weight-training workout after a month layoff would make you a little sore, but soon you would hit your stride again, beginning to regain muscular tone fairly quickly.

Basic Training. By action, I don't mean just going through the motions. The word *action* by definition means something done or affected, the bringing about of an alteration. Movement per se (flailing one's arms about, for example) does not constitute action; action means proceeding. The process of action, in which you are about to become involved through Basic Training, is exactly the process of action that will catapult you beyond any unnecessary fear or hesitation about physical action itself. Now, perhaps you already know all this; perhaps you already know that the best way to overcome fear is to push on in spite of it. But as your coach, as a team coach, I have to assume that some of you need an explanation. So bear with me while I explain what I mean by example.

The imaginary run I just took you through a few pages ago was a successful run. You felt the burning in your legs and the rasping in your throat—that's as bad as it gets—and you got through it. But what if you had stopped at the first sign of discomfort, or anything that seemed unfamiliar? Or what if, like an acquaintance of mine, you never even exerted yourself to the point where it was possible to feel those things?

Let's call this woman Prudence. As a student at Vassar, she lifted weights and ran on the school track team. One day she called me up to announce, "I want to run in next year's New York Marathon. How should I train?" I suggested a six-month running program whereby she could build up in crescendolike fashion for the 26.2-mile event. If, toward the latter end of that six-month period, she was running about 10 miles a day, I would outline a final two months of training.

Six months later Prudence called up to say she was ready to graduate to the next training stage, so we made plans to meet. At the track she told me that after two months of building up to it, she had fixed a routine of running 10 miles a day, five days a week. As I began to time her run that day, I was figuring that after running 10 miles a day for four months, an energetic twenty-one-year-old such as she should have achieved an 8½-minute mile pace easily. But as I watched her plodding around the track, I began to worry. Only moments after she started, her face was contorting pitifully, and from then on she was gasping for breath and crying nonstop. I decided to run with her for a few miles, if only to try to cheer her up. Nothing in particular was wrong, she said, it was just that she felt she couldn't make it, that she was going to die before ever finishing. That was a little extreme, I thought, since at the pace she was running the only thing she could possibly die of before reaching the finish would be old age.

It was taking Prudence twelve minutes to run each mile. She could have easily walked a mile that fast, with no grimacing, no gasping and no crying. After four months of running 10 miles a day, she was still running slower than she could walk. But something more serious was going on than simply a too-slow pace. Prudence was miserable. I tried to encourage her to run more freely, run like she was a child again, run as if she were chasing a dog for frolic. But she kept saying "I can't." And she wouldn't increase her walk-speed running pace one iota.

Needless to say, Prudence did not run the marathon that year—not because she was potentially unable to and not because she didn't want to. She was physically capable of training hard enough, and in her heart was a strong desire. But her mind wouldn't let her do what her body potentially could do, what her heart wanted her to do. Although she is a Phi Beta Kappa, Prudence is a mental marshmallow when it comes to the kind of action necessary for Basic Training.

Just going through the motions of training is not enough. You must push yourself beyond false limitations. You must press against the boundaries that your mind and fear may have constructed around you. In other words, you must press on despite the feeling that you might be taking a risk. Prudence's problem was not physical inability, but rather a mental attitude that would not allow her to sample the unfamiliar. Your own low expectations, lack of confidence or fear of the unknown may cause you to view Basic Training or any physical exercise as risky even when it is not. As a professional athlete, I can assure you Basic Training is not risky. However if you still maintain that it is, then, as your coach, I say, take the risk. You can overcome your fear only through action.

You Are Made for Intensity

Swimmers training for world-class competition adhere to the adage, "There is no gain without pain." But Janet Guthrie, the first woman to face the Indianapolis 500, finds the following policy more to her liking: "Whenever I feel the urge to exercise, I lie down until it goes away." Indeed, Guthrie was so unaccustomed to exercise that she broke her foot doing jumping jacks in her apartment—just one week before she was to test-run her Indy car for the first time in 1976. Despite her aversion to regimented exercise, Guthrie is a determined competitor, able and willing to push her body through the hardships of her high-speed endurance sport. In the 1978 Indy 500 she raced to an excellent eighth-place finish—despite a broken wrist from a fall playing tennis two days before.

Somewhere between training masochism and all-out hedonism is where most of us function best. In fitness training, a certain amount of stress during a workout, and discomfort afterward, are necessary because of the overload principle; that is, when you push physical capacities beyond what feels comfortable, you trigger the physiological processes by which those capacities increase. This is good pain, the discomfort you must transcend in order to tax your body enough to set off the building process. If you let discomfort stop you, then you are licked before you begin. Progress toward physical potential will remain a fantasy.

I would guess that the *single* reason that some women do exercise without losing weight or gaining in fitness is lack of intensity. I hear thirty-year-old women who are just slightly overweight—maybe ten pounds—complain that they walk all day and can't seem to take off the extra pounds. Walking is not enough exercise for a thirty-year-old. Intensity, the only road to burning calories, is paramount. And some discomfort, or stress, some good pain, always accompanies intensity.

Through exertion itself, you will come to know yourself physically and you will learn what is safe, and what is unsafe, stress. At the beginning, the best rule is to follow your instincts and common sense. But remember that you are doing something new and that *unfamiliar* does not always translate into *dangerous*.

What is familiar to me, after all these years, is water. I am not well balanced on land. It may sound silly but when I have gone hiking with friends, climbing up and down a hill that ten-year-olds run up and down with no problem becomes a painstaking effort for me. Most of my weight is in my upper body. I have a very high center of gravity and thus poor balance; my ankles are extremely flexible from swimming and I always fear that a misstep on a rock will twist my foot.

I become tense and afraid of hurting myself because the situation is so foreign to me—although it is not in fact dangerous. Much of Basic Training will be unfamiliar to you. But you will learn that a pounding heart, aching legs and a stitch in your side are not dangerous.

In my 42-hour attempt to swim from Cuba to Florida, I suffered much pain in varying forms—seasickness, jellyfish stings, a right shoulder that throbbed with fatigue. But as the hours passed, as day turned to night, night turned to day, day once more turned to night and night again broke into daylight, the realization of how much discomfort I had already gone through made me feel more and more positive that I could go through what was to come. I amazed myself and that amazement calmed me, assured me that I was capable of absolutely anything. You will experience the same boost from overcoming whatever constitutes a challenge for you.

Be aware of your own signals of fatigue. Overall fatigue, listlessness or lack of interest can make you vulnerable to injury. You shouldn't stop when fatigued, but you should concentrate a little more keenly than usual because your body's reflexes and protection mechanisms may be slower.

I'd again advise a visit to a doctor or to your local Y for a stress test if you are over thirty, if you have not exercised in several years, are seriously overweight or have had any special medical problems. But most women know on their own what parts of their bodies are more susceptible than others to stress. These may be areas of muscular weaknesses or imbalance, structural misalignment, areas of past injury.

Do not, however, favor one leg or arm over the other because of past injury or weakness. *Balanced training is essential.* The point is to be especially responsive to sharp pain in that area if it happens, or to avoid any sport or activity that places a special stress on that area before you have built up sufficient strength.

The myth that females are more prone than males to injury during physical activity has been disproven. Biology is not our dismal destiny: nothing about the female's physiology has made, or ever will make, her as vulnerable to injury as neglect. In fact, with her subcutaneous layer of fat, the female has an extra cushion protecting her. In addition, her sexual machinery, internal as it is, is far more protected than that of the male. In distance swimming, I've always been grateful I'm not a male. Swims sometimes take so much time, up to forty or fifty or sixty straight hours, that a man's beard grows during the swim into a sharp stubble that rubs his shoulder raw and bloody as he continually turns his face toward his shoulder to breathe. Clearly, in ways large and small, it is not always a physical advantage to be male.

These days, because of Title IX, the federal law that mandates equal athletic opportunity in schools, and because of parental attitudes liberalized by the women's movement, a young girl is less likely to grow up a stranger to her own body. Recent statistics on injuries reflect the sociological changes. Scientists have identified a dearth of conditioning and training, and lack of proper facilities and equipment, as the factors causing past discrepancies between female and male injury rates.

To the beginning, as well as to the experienced athlete, accidents do happen: a turned ankle, a strained muscle or ligament, even a broken bone. *But these accidents need never happen* if you take the simple precaution of educating yourself beforehand, following a regimen of consistent and regular warm-ups before training or competition and using common sense. Injuries, when they do happen, need not be debilitating. The science of sports medicine is advancing in this decade as never before, and practitioners have discovered methods of rehabilitation which reduce the convalescence time, as well as the incidence of reinjury.

Where do *you* stand right now? As you get ready to start your Basic Training, you are probably more physically capable than you think. You know that whatever discomfort is involved in intensity won't feel that bad. You know that beginning Basic Training isn't really all that risky; at the same time, the more feelings of risk you overcome at the beginning, the more confident you'll feel at the end.

When You Feel as if You Can't Go On . . . Mental Tricks to Keep Yourself Going

Basic Training is no less a mental challenge than it is a physical one. You'll never know the real extent of your physical strength unless you exercise some mental strength to persevere. It takes willpower to resist that occasional urge to quit before your workout is finished; it takes mental courage to push yourself beyond what is easy into that intensity that makes a workout worthwhile. Whether the obstacle is boredom, fat or discomfort, you can overcome it by a constructive attitude and by trying some of the mental techniques that I use. Here are some tips to keep you going when the going gets tough.

1. Always precede your workout by focusing on your goals. Before you begin, know why you're working out and what results you'll gain. (A glance at the benefits of Basic Training on p. 65 should refresh your motivation.)

2. As you start, remind yourself of the way you must work out for maximum benefit: with intensity, precision and good form. Remember that in aerobics the required *intensity* is signaled by a pulse rate of 80% of 220 minus your age; in weight training, for required intensity use enough weight to make each muscle group exhausted by the twelfth repetition. Keep in mind the importance of *precision*: in aerobics, 15 minutes means not a second less than 15 minutes. In weight training, precision means no less than 12 reps, and *good form* requires a slow and steady squeezing movement of the weights; remember the form in the photographs and concentrate on copying it.

3. Now that you have reminded yourself *why* you're working out and are concentrating on *how*, you can use any or all of the following mental devices to make the time seem to pass more quickly, to get yourself over hurdles of discomfort:

● *Counting:* When you are doing any kind of aerobics, you can count every arm swing or step of your leg and see how many sets of 100 you accumulate in 15 minutes. Or make up intervals. For example, counting one every time your left foot hits the ground, count up to 100. Count while you run 10 steps slowly, then count the next 90 steps as you run them fast, then 10 steps slowly; 80 steps fast and so on. Or pick a number and concentrate on achieving it; as you're moving toward it, concentrate on what part of that goal number you've already achieved. (Counting toward a goal number can become a little race all in itself.) Or, try counting in French or Spanish.

● *Singing:* I sing silently to myself as a variation of counting. Pick a Beatles song or "Row, Row, Row Your Boat" and sing it to the cadence of your stride. (Some people like to wear earphones and listen to music during their workouts.)

● *Focusing:* Focus in on a part of your body for a while. For example, if you're bored or hurting, focus on your stomach muscles and start noticing how hard they're working, how strong they've become. If your calves start hurting when you're skipping rope, focus on your wrists—think about how tiny a circle they can make swinging the handles of the rope. If your arms and shoulders become fatigued, think about your feet—concentrate on skipping lightly on the balls of your feet. When some part of your body is uncomfortable, focus on another part and concentrate on how balanced, relaxed and capable it is. This can make the minutes fly by, take your mind off discomfort and keep you from quitting.

● *Planning:* Use the time to order your life. Think of the things you need to do in the near or the far future, and plan how you're going to do them. If you focus on what you're going to eat that day, you'll probably think of only healthy things like orange juice, salad or a banana. The last thing your hard-working muscles will be craving is a doughnut! Or plan a letter you need to write: Envision how you'd write the first paragraph, then the second and so forth. Another variation of planning out your life is to review what you've experienced so far that day and, if you like, try rerunning the day, this time making the unpleasant things that happened happen another way, a better way, in your mind.

● *Envisioning:* Just as when you focus, you should focus on positive things, when you daydream, always envision constructively. Think how incredible it is that your body can work this well; you're going to have so much energy; you're going to look so great in your clothes. As long as daydreaming doesn't interfere with your concentration, envision the things you've always wanted to do, believing in your capacity to reach your goals. So when you get into the shower after your workout, this vision will stay with you and energize you. Maybe you really will take that photography course you've always wanted to!

● *Challenge the seemingly impossible:* Even if you underestimate yourself now, you can overcome low expectations. Say, you have come to a point (in the 90/90's, for example) where you feel that it's impossible to endure the burning sensation for a second longer. Push it. Stay there for 5 seconds longer. Now you know you have 5 seconds more muscle endurance than you thought you had. The next time you do 90/90's, keep going for at least as long as you did last time; then, and only then, consider if you must the possibility that you can't go on—then go for 5 seconds longer. And so on, the next time, and the time after that. Pretty soon you will have increased the time you thought you could last by at least 30 more seconds. What does that tell you? It tells you that the impossible can be possible. It tells you that you can, if you just will. Every time you master your determination to make a start at something, and gather momentum to follow it through, you make it easier for yourself the next time. Your long-term proof of improvement is that with each subsequent workout, you'll feel less fatigue, less discomfort during the same amount of time. But you don't have to wait for this long-term gratification—you feel gratified the minute each exercise is over because you realize you had the will to see it through.

CHAPTER 2

Aerobic Activity for the Heart and Lungs

Arriving at a clear-cut definition of fitness is not easy, though one thing is certain: *Fitness* does not mean *health,* and vice versa. There are millions of people who are *healthy*—people who are free from disease—but who are overweight, tire easily and cannot physically cope with emergencies. On the other hand, a number of finely tuned athletes suffer from temporary or even chronic ill-health. Studies from the last ten Olympic Games reveal that many of the gold medal winners performed with colds, flus, allergies and even more serious problems such as pneumonia and broken bones. So on a day-to-day basis, fitness and health may not be the same thing. But on a *long-term* basis, notwithstanding diet, personal habits such as smoking and hereditary predisposition toward certain diseases, fitness *is* a close cousin to good health. If you can achieve fitness—low pulse rate, low body-fat percentage, strength and flexibility of the muscles and joints—consistent good health has a better chance of following.

The President's Council on Physical Fitness and Sports defines fitness as "the ability to carry out daily tasks with vigor and alertness, without undue fatigue, and with ample energy to enjoy leisure time pursuits and to meet unforeseen emergencies." To become fit is to sharpen and make efficient the physiological processes.

To become fit is to pursue four major goals. They are:

1. Strengthen the cardiovascular system and lower the resting pulse rate.
2. Keep body-fat percentage within acceptable limits.
3. Give strength and endurance to the skeletal muscles.
4. Increase flexibility of the skeletal muscles and joints.

Each of these four components is necessary to total fitness. If you keep all of them at satisfactory levels, you will enjoy greater reserves of energy for physical, emotional and intellectual activities. You will be blessed with rewarding sleep, better digestion, greater resistance to most common illnesses (like colds and flu), and, I maintain, you will think better of yourself. In other words, if these four basic fitness goals are pursued, general good health and high self-esteem will almost certainly follow.

How do you best go about attaining these four physiological goals? The key to the most important ones—the first two—is your heart.

Here I must introduce some basic physiology, for it is important for you to understand how the heart, lungs and muscles function in order to know how to make them perform their best. As you approach your first day of Basic Training, you should appreciate why aerobic exercises designed to strengthen the heart, the lungs and the rest of the oxygen-transport system make up a major part of my Basic Training schedule.

The heart is a hollow mass of contractile muscle about the size of a clenched fist. The heart functions as the originator in a transport system: It pumps pure blood from the left ventricle, through the aorta, to all the cells of the body except those in the lungs. After this blood has nourished the cells and received their waste products, the impure blood is drawn through the veins back to the right auricle of the heart. From here it passes into the right ventricle where it receives oxygen and is purified. The blood is carried back through the pulmonary veins to the left auricle. The pure blood then enters the left ventricle and the cycle begins again. In the average person, this miraculous process is carried out approximately 72 times a minute for approximately 72 years.

You may be wondering about the old wives' tale that each heart has a certain quota of beats during a lifetime—and if you speed up the heartbeat with vigorous exercise, you will more quickly use up your quota. The truth is just the opposite. A heart that is always at rest is smaller, weaker and more burdened than a heart that has been consistently and reasonably stressed. My Basic Training is designed to help you reach that level of consistent and reasonable stress most beneficial to your heart.

A heart that receives no strenuous exercise will be like any other unused muscle: inefficient and weak. It will be able to handle only small volumes of blood and will have to beat more quickly to transport needed blood throughout the body. During work it will struggle to pump the additionally needed volume of blood through contracted and inelastic vessels. Regular vigorous exercise improves this performance dramatically. The organ becomes more powerful through practice; if the heart is regularly filled with the large volume of blood demanded by the muscles during exercise, and powerfully forced to squeeze that extra blood supply back to the muscles, it becomes capable of a more powerful contraction. Similarly, the cardio-vascular vessels expand and grow more flexible with the pressure of the increased volume. Some scientists believe that even *collateral* circulation—circulation through an added capillary network both in and around the heart and around the blood vessels of a well-exercised individual—is possible. At rest, therefore, the exercised heart can beat more slowly because each beat can transport a larger volume of blood. A well-conditioned heart with greater heart muscle efficiency and a well-developed capillary network is more likely to survive a heart attack and is less prone to fatal attacks.

Another added efficiency in the circulatory system that comes with regular strenuous exercise occurs in the blood itself. Platelets, which carry the blood-clotting mechanisms, along with the red corpuscles and the white cells, are the solid elements of the blood visible under an ordinary microscope. In sedentary individuals, platelets can become sticky and clog vessels in the brain and heart, resulting in strokes and heart attacks. With even mild exercise, the platelet aggregation is decreased.

The type of exercise that best develops the heart and the oxygen transport system is rhythmic and continuous. Such training increases the maximum oxygen uptake (the volume of oxygen that an individual can use in one minute). And the continual exercises that best serve to increase this maximum oxygen intake are called *aerobic*, meaning *with oxygen*.

You will see that Basic Training, while much concerned with strength and flexibility, is *most* concerned with aerobics. Because I have been a swimmer all my life, and because swimming is a continuous, oxygen-demanding exercise, I have developed my oxygen-transport to its ultimate potential. My heart has become so efficient that its resting pulse has been below 40 beats per minute. My lung capacity is 6.2 liters, which a few years ago was larger than any player on the New York Jets football team—and I am only 5'6", 130 pounds. In other words, my heart at rest has very little work to do.

Exercise may loosely be defined as movement that requires exertion. The *muscles* are the instruments that produce this movement. Muscular contraction is not a particularly simple concept, in physiological terms, but a brief analysis will help show why aerobic exercise is the most efficient type of exercise for the heart.

The trick to muscular contraction lies in converting chemical energy into mechanical energy, or movement. We are looking for an equation in which a reaction takes place using the glycogen, a usable simple sugar in your food, and yields energy as a by-product. For example, a simplified version of such an equation for muscular contraction is: A carbon compound such as glucose reacts with oxygen to produce carbon dioxide, water and energy. Because this particular metabolic process requires oxygen, it is an aerobic process. Another energy-yielding process occurs when glucose reacts with a fragment of another carbon compound, without oxygen, to produce energy with lactic acid (a waste product). This process is *anaerobic*.

An anaerobic exercise must be intense and short enough in duration so that oxygen is not required—a 15-second, all-out sprint on a bicycle, or a 30-second sprint in a pool, or perhaps a 1-minute 440 around the track. All these endeavors will raise the pulse in response to a greater glycogen demand. None requires excessive amounts of oxygen or will tax the oxygen-transport system because they don't continue long enough. For this reason, anaerobic exercise cannot best improve the maximum oxygen intake, one of the most important steps toward fitness.

The aerobic process *does* require a great deal of oxygen. If you were to bicycle for 3 minutes, swim for 15 minutes, or run for 30 minutes, the muscle cells would need oxygen to combine with glucose or glycogen to produce energy. This energy would be converted to mechanical energy as the exercise continued. In other words, it is not simply a question of raising the pulse to 140 beats a minute for 10 minutes a day—being extremely frightened 10 times a day would do nothing for the cardiovascular system because the muscles would not demand excess oxygen and the oxygen-transport system would not be taxed. The skeletal muscles must work together with the heart; the entire oxygen-transport system must be in effect.

As you begin Basic Training, you will notice that I am adamant about which exercises you may do as the aerobic component of your workout. You *must* choose among *swimming, running, rowing, cycling, skipping rope* and *cross-country skiing*—though you can alternate your choice daily, if you want. This is not to say that an afternoon of soccer or several sets of singles tennis will not serve to stimulate the oxygen-transport system. They will, but not as quickly and as consistently as the purely continuous aerobic exercises listed above. It is no coincidence that the greatest cross-country skiers, swimmers, runners, cyclists and rowers have lower average resting pulses, higher maximum oxygen intakes, lower body-fat percentages and larger lung capacities than the greatest basketball and tennis players. And, in general, the same results will hold true for you. If you stick with Basic Training aerobics, your cardiovascular and pulmonary systems will become stronger and more efficient in 6 months than if you did any other sport or activity for a full year.

Now that we've seen how aerobic exercise can sharpen the first physiological process toward fitness—strengthen the cardiovascular system and lower the resting pulse rate—how can it sharpen the second? (How can it keep the body-fat percentage at low levels?)

Once and for all you should accept the fact that some fat is essential to every human being, male and female. Fat serves as a long-term storage vault for energy, while providing insulation for the body and protection for the delicate inner organs. But what is a *desirable* amount of fat? It is not *how much* fat an individual has that is important, but *what percentage* of the total body weight is fat. The average body composition for an adult man in the United States today includes 15 to 19 percent fat; and the average woman's body is 22 to 26 percent fat. Though obesity is clinically defined as a body with more than 30 percent fat content, the current averages for both men and women are still considered overfat. Ideal would be under 12 percent for men, under 18 percent for women—as an average. How can you tell how much of your weight is fat? A good everyday measurement is the mirror check. For me, a close inspection for firm muscle tone at every angle in a full-length mirror is a much better indicator of fat than a moment on the scales. Or the pinch test will do: pinch (vertically) the excess skin at the side of your waist. If more than an inch of flesh is held between your fingers, you know there is fat to be lost and muscle to be toned. And especially check your buttocks and the outsides of your thighs. I realize these areas are extremely difficult for us women to make perfectly smooth and firm. But if the dimples are evident here you are not burning enough calories in your aerobic workouts— or you're eating too fatty a diet of sugar, dairy products and red meat (see the Diet Primer, p. 179).

I usually consider 130 pounds a good weight for me. At this weight, I'm not skinny as a model, but I'm trim and lean. Yet I have been 130 pounds with 15.5 percent fat on my body. I can see the fleshiness in the mirror and people say, "You're a bit heavy these days, aren't you?" On the other hand, I have been 138 pounds with 9.8 percent of my body as fat, seeing nothing but solid muscle in the mirror, and people say, "Gee, you're thin these days, aren't you?" Muscle is *always* preferable to fat, whether for looks or for health.

Keep in mind that the bathroom scale can sometimes mislead. Your weight is a good indication of your fat percentage but not an accurate measurement. *Muscle weighs more than fat,* but it is, nevertheless, more desirable. Muscle is dense, active tissue, while fat is inert tissue. Extra fat is a parasite. It makes demands on the heart for oxygen and nutrients but it does no work in return; it saps valuable life supply that is needed by the involuntary muscles, the skeletal muscles and even the necessary minimum amount of fat. Extra fat also causes friction between lean muscle fibers and makes muscular contraction less efficient.

The only way to get rid of excess fat is exercise, and the type of exercise that burns the most fat in the least time is aerobic. As the muscles are asked to perform continual, intense work, they demand a steady flow of glycogen to produce movement. As the usable glycogen that was available before exercise began is depleted, the stored fat reserve provides additional glycogen until exercise ceases. Fat is burned in this way.

For me, aerobic exercise has always been the key to weight control. Women always drool with envy as I finish my third dessert at dinner. They say, "Oh, you're so lucky to be able to eat whatever you want!" Luck, actually, has very little to do with it. I can and do eat three desserts after dinner when I am training eight hours a day. But when I am in the off-season, going at it strenuously about four hours a day, I have to cut down on the sweets and carbohydrates. And I have even experienced brief periods in my life, usually because of injury, when I have had to be virtually inactive—I could walk and perform all the daily tasks of a business woman or a mother but I couldn't run or play hard at anything. And I have learned during these periods, almost to my surprise, that I am like any other woman—without any regular strenuous exercise in my life, I must allow myself a fairly small food intake in order to prevent weight gain. And more important than the amount of food is the quality of food. I try to eliminate all sugar and almost all fat (I indulge in an occasional yogurt or steak) when I am unable to exercise intensely.

One day I will no longer be participating in such a strenuous sport. I will be putting all of my energy into career and family and social life. At that time I will turn to Basic Training—and a sugar-free, low-fat diet. The aerobics and weight-training of Basic Training will force you to burn enough calories and develop enough muscle so that your body-fat percentage will be ideal.

The Basics of Aerobic Training

Remember that the two methods of exercise to burn energy (measured in calories) are anaerobic and aerobic. While the intensity of an anaerobic workout can potentially burn more fat than an aerobic workout of the same duration, the anaerobic workout will cause more immediate fatigue and keep you from performing again until there has been sufficient rest. An aerobic workout can last an almost unlimited time and can be done every day, even twice a day.

Consider this example: If you are riding a stationary bicycle at a given tension (resistance level of the pedals) and you sprint as hard as you possibly can for 30 seconds, your pulse rate will soar dramatically and you will burn a high number of calories—many more than 30 seconds of semi-intense riding at the same tension at a slightly lower pulse rate. But because neither your heart nor your legs will be able to handle that kind of all-out sprinting for very long, you will need to rest and recover before you can go all out again. A series of these all-out sprints in one workout results in a buildup of waste products (lactic acid) in the muscles which will make you too sore and fatigued to perform at such intensity until rest has allowed such waste products to be flushed out of the muscles. I have a friend on the professional racquetball tour who is very strong and in quite good shape; she can only perform five 30-second sprints on the bike before she is too wasted to go another. Then, she must rest at least 24 hours, sometimes longer, before she is able to perform the series of 5 sprints again at full throttle. On the other hand, she is in good enough shape to go 20 minutes on the bike nonstop at slightly less intensity twice a day. So in terms of burning calories, which workout makes sense—the anaerobic, which is only two and a half minutes of work and cannot be repeated for a day or two, or the aerobic, which is 20 minutes of work and can be repeated the same day?

Many studies show that the submaximal work of a 70–75 percent effort aerobic workout will produce the same caloric expenditure of a maximal 95–100 percent effort anaerobic workout when the exercise time is of the same duration. In other words, a half-hour run at 75 percent effort may burn the same amount of calories as a half-hour of anaerobic sprint runs with necessary rest between efforts. (Lactic acid will also be produced during aerobic activity—when oxygen becomes scarce—but not in the same volume as during anaerobic activity.)

Aerobics are the answer. But even the best aerobic exercise will do very little for you if performed at a minimum level of exertion. Jogging too slowly or gently splashing up and down a pool are wastes of time. As each individual's resting pulse and maximum heart rate (the highest the pulse will go during intense exercise) varies from another's, so does the optimum pulse rate at which to perform an aerobic workout.

A good, useful pulse rate during an aerobic workout is *80 percent of 220 MINUS YOUR AGE*. For example, the optimum workout pulse rate for a thirty-year-old is 80 percent of 220 minus 30, or 152. And the optimum type of exercise to keep your pulse rate at this level throughout a workout is one that requires several large muscle groups demanding oxygenated blood from the heart.

To be sure, continuous disco dancing or active sex could qualify and, if we used our imaginations we could invent new forms of exercise that would meet the requirements. You don't have to jog to be aerobically fit. To be aerobically fit you can do any daily exercise that can be done nonstop for at least 15 minutes, which maintains your pulse at 80 percent of 220 minus your age for those 15 minutes. (You may not be able to do a full 15 minutes of aerobic exercise when you start, but you will work up to a higher level.) It just so happens that the proven aerobic exercises are easily measured in all those necessary terms and thus qualify without question—running, swimming, cross-country skiing, rowing, skipping rope and cycling. Choose one or more of these exercises to make up the aerobic part of your Basic Training. Again, *no other* sport or activity may be substituted for any of these six. What follows is a brief comparison of these aerobic activities.

Take Your Time!

Basic Training starts with a few minutes of stretching and a couple of minutes of warm-up before the 15 minutes of high-pulse aerobics. You don't just jump from a few minutes of stretching right up to 80 percent of 220 minus your age. This would be too sudden a jolt. Take 2 full minutes, at the least, to gradually build your pulse rate before you reach the magic goal number—before you start counting the 15 minutes. And the best way to raise your pulse rate is to start your chosen aerobic activity at an extremely slow rate. After a minute or so, move to a moderate pace; after 2 minutes you will probably be ready to slip up to your desirable pulse and start counting the 15 minutes.

1. SWIMMING

Swimming, unique among all sports and exercises, demands work from every muscle in the body. The only equipment needed is a suit, goggles and, of course, water. Highly developed skills are not necessary. As long as you can swim continuously for at least 15 minutes, you will derive all the aerobic benefits of Basic Training. Incidence of injury in swimming is almost nonexistent. Except for occasional shoulder bursitis in full-time competitive swimmers, injuries are rare because the water cushions and protects the joints and muscles.

If you were to experiment with all six aerobic activities, let's say one year of strenuous devotion to each one, one at a time, you would find that your body-fat percentage would remain highest while swimming. Swimmers' bodies usually reserve a layer of adipose tissue for insulation and buoyancy so that even world-class swimmers at their leanest appear slightly soft and fleshy compared to steely muscled cyclists and skiers. On the other hand, I have found an obvious answer for every woman who has complained to me that although she is swimming regularly she is unable to lose weight. I go to her pool to observe her workout and, inevitably, I find that she is lollygagging up and down instead of concentrating on heavy exertion every lap. When the swimming season comes around for me, I lose weight and fat percentage immediately as I start to pour on the intensity.

The sweat won't be as obvious a sign of hard work as while skipping rope, for instance, but you will definitely be sweating if you're swimming hard. Don't get in there and do an Esther Williams sidestroke up and down, afraid to splash up a lot of white water. Don't do a dainty breaststroke, afraid to get your hair wet. Breaststroke is okay for competitive swimmers who understand the difficult technique necessary to get a good workout, but for you, freestyle (crawl) or backstroke are the two choices. Warm-up doesn't count toward your 15 intense minutes, conversation with the lifeguard doesn't count, stopping at the end of the pool between laps doesn't count. Every time you push off the wall for another lap, try to get to the other end

as fast as possible, as if you were in a race.

If you have access to a lake or ocean for part or all of the year, the cardinal rule is that you swim *parallel* to not away from, the shore. When at all possible, swim with someone, or have a friend or a lifeguard nearby on shore look out for you. At the very least, be aware of the water temperature, the jellyfish and the man-of-war situation; and the various currents, riptides, low-tide times; and nature of the bottom (coral, sea urchins and so on). Clean ocean or lake water is much healthier than a chlorinated pool. Also, your workout can be more continually efficient because you never have to stop for a turn. The big disadvantage in open-water swimming is keeping on course. I can swim for hours along a shoreline without ever breaking stroke by simply glancing up now and then, but this skill comes only with experience. If you must stop fully to look around and get your bearings and defog your goggles, it will interrupt the required continuity of your workout; you cannot count these stops in your 15 minutes. Moreover, I find that intensity is more difficult to maintain in open-water swimming. You tend to daydream, whereas swimming in a pool forces you to keep up your thinking into fast laps.

2. RUNNING

You can run outdoors on any type of surface almost any day of the year. But on severe winter days, a stationary treadmill or an indoor track at your school or the local Y will serve nicely until you can return to the open spaces. A high degree of skill is not necessary for cardiovascular conditioning. Style is not critical; if you can run for at least 15 continuous minutes, you can improve your aerobic fitness level dramatically.

Style *does* count in terms of possible injuries, however, for poor form can initiate tendon, cartilage, nerve and bone problems in the knees, the hip, the back, the shins and the feet. As a matter of fact, running with good or even perfect form is often not an injury-free situation. The knee, especially, must absorb hundreds of pounds of pressure each

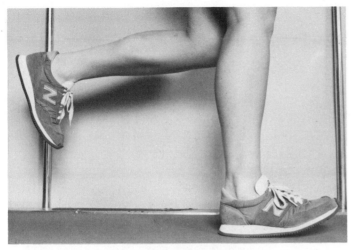

time one foot hits the ground—a pressure that the knees are not designed to absorb.

Let me give you a few general tips on form. One, step lightly so that you can barely hear your sneakers touch the ground. Two, let your heel hit the ground first, and then roll onto the ball of your foot and finally push off for the next step with your toes. Three, keep your legs and feet parallel, so that your feet don't turn in or out. Four, bend your knees very slightly and lean forward from the waist very slightly, so that if you were to run an imaginary pole down through your body from your neck to your feet, it would touch almost every part—except your knees and your shoulders which would be just a few inches in front of the pole. Five, relax your upper body by letting your shoulders hang loosely and by holding your elbows in loosely at your waist and your hands loosely straight out in front of your waist—wrists limp. Don't clench your fists or shrug your shoulders. Six, think of moving *forward* as opposed to *up and down*—throw each foot out in front of you, lengthening your stride, instead of lifting each foot high off the ground.

If you are going to choose running as one of your regular Basic Training exercises, get a good pair of shoes, with enough cushioning for shock absorption. The expense is well worth it. Running magazines give comparative ratings of all the recent models, and most sales people at running equipment stores can give you expert advice on the right model for you.

Stretching is a daily requirement of Basic Training. But you should spend a few more minutes a day before running outdoors in cold weather. Also, always opt for grass or dirt or even cinder before asphalt (but take asphalt before concrete). The combination of good shoes, good form, proper stretching and avoidance of hard surfaces should help you avoid minor as well as major injuries. If your shins ache (shin splints) or your knees or hips ache, take a few days off and come back with better-cushioned sneakers or move to a more giving surface. If you experience a knifelike pain anywhere, especially the knee, consult a sports-oriented doctor immediately.

The only major disadvantage to running is that the muscles of the upper body—the shoulders, chest and arms—are somewhat neglected. Except during high-intensity sprints, where upper-body strength and a powerful pumping action of the arms are required, your upper body is under little or no stress.

A unique phenomenon occurs in runners. Regular distance runners—those putting in at least 50 miles per week—seem to register a consistently lower body-fat percentage than participants putting in the equivalent amount of time in another aerobic activity. All six of the basic aerobic exercises burn calories very efficiently, but running lowers body-fat percentage more quickly than the others.

Running with a friend or a group can make the time pass quickly and can be a wise safety precaution at night or early in the morning. However, I don't buy those long-winded conversations while you're working out. If you have enough breath to talk while you run, your intensity level is way out of line. Give your workout all the concentration it warrants and save the socializing for later.

3. CYCLING

Technique, while important to competitive cyclists, is not an issue when cycling for aerobic fitness. You don't need an expensive imported bicycle, and you don't need toe clips or special cleated shoes. If you can pedal continuously and intensely on any bicycle or stationary bicycle for at least 15 minutes, you will give your cardiovascular system an excellent workout. Ride in high gear (harder to pedal) to build more leg muscle; ride in low gear (easier to pedal) for a quicker turnover and greater stimulus to the heart—but don't make the pedaling so easy that your feet spin around out of control and don't make it so hard that you have to grunt and strain to grind out one revolution of the pedals.

Competitive sprinters and experienced road racers use the upper body extensively. Manipulation of the handlebars through upper-body strength allows the legs extra leverage. But for recreational and fitness cyclists, the lower back, the abdominals, the quadriceps (especially), the hamstrings and the calves expend a tremendous effort while the upper body is relatively neglected, as in running. (Your buttocks will work harder if you lower the seat.)

Cyclists suffer occasional knee problems but the incidence of all leg and back injuries is much rarer in their case than it is for runners. If you choose cycling, make sure your seat height is at a level so that your leg is just slightly bent when your foot hits the lowest point in the revolution. Your knee should never lock—and you should press the pedal with the ball of the foot, not with your toes or your heel. Although this is the ideal seat height, I occasionally lower my seat when working out on a stationary bike in order to give my buttocks some extra work.

Go the whole 15 minutes as if you were in a race. Bear down on the pedals with intensity so that you start sweating heavily within 2 minutes of starting. If 15 minutes seem like an eternity at this tough pace—and they should if you're working hard enough—do counting tricks to pass the time, like counting to 100, counting each time your left foot presses the pedal and then counting to 90, then 80, and so on. This way each number goal will seem easier and keep you occupied until, before you know it, 15 minutes will have passed. Or get a set of stereo headphones and tune in to an upbeat station. This is what I sometimes do during my stationary bike workouts.

Good bicycles are not terribly expensive to begin with, but a number of accessories—protective helmet, sturdy lock, night-lights—are advisable. There are plenty of suitable routes for bicycles in

rural and suburban America—even the big cities are opening bike lanes. (Smog masks might be advisable in big cities.) And the bicycle gets more miles per gallon than any other vehicle on the road.

There are also several brands of excellent stationary bicycles available today. Either purchase one—just make sure the seat is a comfortable style for you and make sure there is a guarantee on the tension-control mechanism—or use one at your health club, Y or school. You can perform exactly the same aerobic workout on a stationary bike as on a road bike. In some ways, a stationary bike is better because you won't have to look for a course free of any obstacles that might interrupt your continuous workout. You won't be limited by weather or by auto exhaust fumes. And a stationary bike will take up only 16 square feet in your home or office.

I am an ardent fan of the stationary bike for the ultimate in an efficient and convenient workout, but I rarely find people who know how to use the bike to its potential. At my health club there was a woman who would show up Sunday mornings with the entire Sunday *New York Times*, park herself on one of the few bikes, and proceed to read the paper front to back as she pedaled for two hours at a snail's pace. After witnessing this alarming waste of time and machinery for a few weeks, I decided to interrupt her in the middle of the Arts and Leisure section and politely offer her a quick lecture on physiology and its response to intensity. The following Sunday she rode at breakneck speed for 15 minutes, climbed off the bike dripping wet and breathing very hard, stretched for a few minutes before her shower and read her *Times* over a tall glass of carrot juice at the health club bar. Don't even bother to climb into the saddle if you're not willing to finish up with legs burning and clothes wringing wet.

4. SKIPPING ROPE

It used to be that only little girls and boxers skipped rope. Today, jump ropes made of leather, cloth and plastic have become the inexpensive tools for many fitness enthusiasts. Leather will last longer—but make sure the handles are the ball-bearing variety so that rope won't fray with each revolution. All you need is a floor space of 10' x 5' and a ceiling about 3' higher than your own height. Skipping outside on the pavement or on the lawn is possible. Skipping indoors is preferable, however, as the surface will be more even and will allow you to develop rhythm and consistent speed, and wind and weather problems obviously will be eliminated. Skipping on a rug will develop extra strength in the calves because they must drive the feet high out of the soft cushion in order to keep you from stepping on the rope; but skipping on a rug

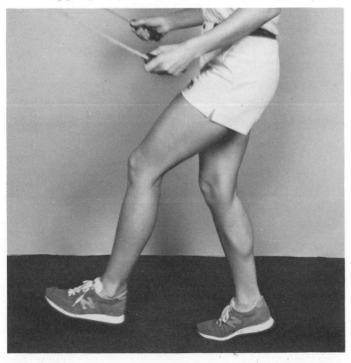

often interrupts continuity because the rope catches on the rug fibers instead of gliding as it does over hard surfaces. Skipping injuries can include shin splints and aching under the patella (the knee cap). Continuous landing on ungiving concrete jars the lower leg until something must give—and it is rarely the floor. Try to find wood or another surface with "give." Wear well-cushioned shoes.

Skipping demands heavy work from the calves, the deltoids (shoulders) and the forearms; and light, toning work from the upper leg (both quadriceps and hamstrings), the buttocks, the abdominals, the pectorals, the lats (see the muscles outlined on pp. 48–49)and the biceps. In other words, skipping rope is a decent muscular workout as well as an excellent aerobic exercise. Once you get up to a whole 15-minute workout with a rope, your shoulders and forearms should ache at the end, not your calves (unless you're working on a rug). Shoulder endurance is developed while skipping.

Unlike running and swimming, skipping rope requires coordination and good technique in order to qualify as a top aerobic workout. If you step on the rope too often and cannot maintain a quick, continuous rhythm, you cannot fulfill the basic principle of aerobics—CONTINUOUS exercise at a minimum pulse rate of 80 percent of 220 minus your age. Hold the handles waist high, just about one foot from either side of your waist. The wrist action should make tiny circles instead of making large circles by circling your whole forearm. Do not jump high in the air. Three inches off the ground is ideal—one foot at a time or both feet together, swinging the rope over each time you touch the floor. Don't take two jumps for every rope swing as you did when you were a kid. If you are having trouble breaking the two-jump habit, focus on your work. The wrists should snap crisply each time the toes bounce to bring the rope over rapidly. Get the rhythm without the rope, bouncing continuously and quickly without the two-jump/pause routine. The rope is the proper length for you if the top of its arc is passing about one foot over your head as you skip. Proper length is crucial. If your rope is too long, tie knots near the handles; if it's too short, you're in trouble. These tips should help you to develop a smooth technique.

Believe it or not, skipping rope is by far the toughest of these six aerobic activities to do intensely for the continuous 15 minutes. I would bet money that any reasonably fit athlete who does none of these activities regularly could go out on the first day and put in 15 minutes of continuous hard work at the other five—but not skipping rope. So don't be discouraged if you can't do it the first day. It may take as long as six months to put together 15 minutes, even in intervals. Start by doing 100 jumps, rest 30 seconds, and repeat 10 times. If you step on the rope, don't become annoyed; immediately pick up your count where you left off. Once you can perform this 1,000-jump workout with relative ease, do fifteen 1 minute periods (at a pace faster than 100 jumps per minute—my pace is 160 jumps per minute) with 30 seconds rest between each. Start putting together workouts like 3 minutes hard, rest 30 seconds, and so on, for the 15. You will get 15 continuous minutes a few months down the road.

5. ROWING

Competitive rowers with good technique demand about 60 percent of their strength from their legs, 20 percent from the backs and 20 percent from their arms. In other words, when performed properly, rowing is a strenuous workout for all the major muscle groups of the body. Inexperienced rowers, however, try to do all the work with their arms. They have to learn to move the dead, or still, water at the beginning of the stroke, with their legs. In any case, regardless of level of experience or technique, rowing is an excellent continuous exercise for the heart.

The big problem with rowing is accessibility. Very few people have regular access to a shell, a boathouse or a convenient and safe body of water. Consequently, the majority of rowers in the United States today are collegiate competitors. Paddling, which includes all forms of canoeing and kayaking, is found more often than rowing outside the university level but, in terms of mass public participation, it is equally inaccessible.

The same companies that make stationary bi-

cycles make stationary rowing machines. So if you opt for a stationary rowing machine, just make sure you have some guarantee on the tension mechanism. The ergometer can be adjusted according to desired resistance, and the seat should slide with each stroke so that your legs get just as tough a workout as your back, your abdominals and all of your upper body. Like the cycling ergometer, a rowing machine takes up very little space and can provide you with the same aerobic workout as a two-mile outing on the Charles. If you cannot locate a machine at your health spa or local Y, you can purchase one for between $200 and $300.

Rowing on an ergometer or in a shell can be a jerky operation and the rower may be subject to muscle pulls in the quadriceps, the lower back or the shoulders. Make sure you are properly stretched and warmed up before you begin rowing.

6. CROSS-COUNTRY SKIING

When sophisticated athletes in all the aerobic sports are tested and compared in terms of pulse-recovery rate, vital capacity (lung capacity), maximum oxygen uptake and other indications of cardiovascular fitness, cross-country skiers seem to finish consistently higher than swimmers, runners, cyclists or rowers. (And these last four groups finish consistently higher than all other athletes.) The catch here is that the tremendous cardiovascular benefits of cross-country skiing are fully available only to experts who have developed an efficient and skillful style. Regardless of how poor a swimmer, runner or cyclist you are, your continuous and intense effort throughout a workout is directly correlated to your aerobic gain from that workout. But until you master the push-and-glide rhythm of cross-country skiing, your inefficient style will naturally limit the amount of energy you will be able to expend continuously with intensity. Or I should say the amount of the right type of energy. My first time out on skis I put all my energy into the tension of falling, getting up, concentrating on what to do with my skis and my poles, worrying about hitting trees and so on. Now that I'm getting the hang of it,

I can relax and try to get up some speed and actually run/slide on the snow. As you become smoother and better coordinated in your style, you will be able to put as much energy as you need to into your workout. Experience is paramount.

Cross-country skiing is obviously not as accessible as running, swimming, cycling or skipping rope. You must live in a cold climate, which eliminates at least two seasons of the year (although New Yorkers cross-country ski in Central Park in summer on roller-skated skis). And you must have skis, boots, poles, warm clothing—more than the bare essentials of a bathing suit or a pair of running shoes.

If you can come by the equipment, the snow and the experience, however, cross-country skiing is a fine aerobic exercise that neglects very few of the skeletal muscles. All parts of the legs, and especially the quadriceps, the lower back, the abdominals, the arms, the chest and the shoulders are under constant exertion. And you should finish your session dripping wet just as if you'd finished a run in the summer. Be prepared to get out of your wet clothes immediately.

I would highly recommend a couple of lessons for technique; otherwise, you will probably never get the aerobic potential out of cross-country skiing. You should be able, literally, to run on your skis.

Your Pulse Is the Key

As I will suggest later, you should choose one or all of the above activities to satisfy your Basic Training aerobic schedule. Before Day #1 and thereafter for the rest of your life, the best and easiest way to measure your aerobic fitness is your pulse. The two important times to take your pulse are when it is resting, and when it is working hard.

To know your resting pulse, take your resting pulse for one full minute once a week before getting out of bed in the morning. *Record it*. You'll know you are making gains in aerobic fitness and health if the pulse lowers month by month and eventually levels out. You may notice a rise for the first few weeks until your body gets used to the hard work; don't worry—it will drop and it will level

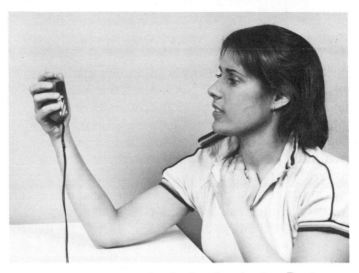

out. If your resting pulse before beginning Basic Training is 82, and if after six months of regular work it is 70, be satisfied to know that your heart is performing under much less strain.

I stay in fairly good shape during the off-season (winter for my sport) with a resting pulse of about 55. When I get down to serious spring training for the summer's long swims, my first month or so of hard work is reflected in a rise in resting pulse to about 65 beats a minute. The tissue needs extra nourishment by the blood to rehabilitate. But by the end of the second month of hard work, all systems have recuperated and benefited from the vigorous pumping—my resting pulse registers in the low 40s and occasionally below 40. With regular participation in Basic Training, you should be able to get your resting pulse down to 62 or lower—at least 10 beats under the national average. Check with your physician if your resting pulse is above 80 after six months of Basic Training. You might have a genetic predisposition toward a high pulse rate or a slight medical problem.

The second time to record your pulse is during the aerobic activity itself. Once in a while, say every two weeks, stop in the middle of your exercise to check your pulse. Count it for only 6 seconds and multiply by ten to get the minute; otherwise, the immediate heart recovery rate will mask the peak exercise heart rate. In other words, if you take your pulse for 6 seconds in the middle of a stationary bike workout and come up with a count of 16, your rate/minute is 16 x 10, or 160. This will be an accurate indication of your peak exercise pulse rate, whereas taking your pulse for thirty or sixty seconds will allow your heart to recover and your pulse will slow down while you are counting it. If your pulse is below 80 percent of 220 minus your age, you know the pace or the intensity of your workout is not sufficient. Don't forget that 80 percent of 220 minus your age is the absolute *minimum* guideline for your working pulse. If you can work at a continuous higher pulse, all the better. At thirty-two years of age, I try to shoot for a pulse rate of at least 180 during my aerobics, which is almost 96 percent of 220 minus 32. You should shoot for the highest percent of your number you can attain without sacrificing continuity—even higher than 100 percent is possible if you can keep your pulse higher than 220 minus your age.

Enjoy aerobics. Some of my happiest moments have been all alone, cherishing an accomplished aerobic workout. The first time I ran 12 miles under 72 minutes, I was prouder than after many of the world records I broke in swimming. I was with a friend at the track, gazing at my stopwatch through tears. And the first time I skipped rope for a continuous hour was a strange moment. I was skipping fairly fast on a squash court, looking out the glass door at a clock. After 22 minutes, I began to feel nauseated. After half an hour, I developed a severe stitch in the left side of my abdomen. I tried breathing deeper but it wouldn't quit. A few minutes later I had a cramp in the right foot. By 50 minutes I was shaking all over and the sweat was so thick in my eyes I had to jerk my head to see the hands of the clock. The second hand approached the hour and when I finished I felt I had been through an emotionally rewarding experience. I was high for a week. It wasn't that I enjoyed the pain. It was that I had refused to give up when I knew I needed the workout to prepare myself for a difficult long swim.

I am neither a professional runner nor a professional rope skipper; I have no intention of competing at either activity. These moments were strictly personal and you will cherish your own personal achievements. You are not a professional athlete training for world-class competition, so you won't have to run or skip as long as I do to achieve that high feeling. But you will feel proud and emotionally satisfied as you become experienced with Basic Training. There will be moments when you will be faced with minor physical discomforts; you will refuse to give up when you know you need to finish the workout to prove to yourself that it's not too much for you. After all, if you give up once, giving up might become a habit. You will come to know your body—your heart, your muscles—and you will extend your aerobics beyond the minimum intensity of 80 percent of 220 minus your age. And eventually, the harder you push, the more magnificently your body will respond. Suddenly, things that used to be such a struggle—like walking home with a heavy bag of groceries or climbing five flights of stairs—will become a breeze.

CHAPTER 3

The Muscles

No longer do we have to listen to rantings about how physical activity is detrimental to childbirth, about how the menstrual cycle detracts from athletic performance or about how a woman's weak bone structure makes her particularly vulnerable to injury. Indeed, more and more studies tell us that regular, sensible exercise makes childbirth easier, that menstrual cramps are less severe for women who exercise (many women have broken world records during menstruation), that the differences in bone mass and density between men and women are negligible with respect to potential bone breakage and that, in fact, the woman's natural extra layer of fat serves to better protect her against damage to bones and delicate organs.

Many myths have been debunked in recent years, though one continues to survive: that a woman who pursues muscular development is somehow "not feminine," that she is not really a "woman." And while many of you very feminine women have left the vibrating belts for sophisticated weight-training machines, I get the distinct impression you're not sure why, and that you worry that your increased muscular development can only harm you—physically, socially, or both.

I must warn you at this point—before you edge even one page nearer to actual workouts—that weight training is absolutely *crucial* to my Basic Training. Weights are not thrown into Basic Training merely to break up a regular aerobic routine. The weight program is here to help you achieve muscle tone, a lower fat percentage and a stronger body overall. Keep an open mind. Read through this chapter to learn why overall muscular stimula-

tion is a major part of fitness, to learn how to use weights properly and discover (to your relief) that you couldn't build *huge* muscle mass even if you wanted to.

Why has society looked unfavorably on muscles on women? Does the thought of a woman developing her strength threaten the male's assumed physical superiority? *Is* a man superior, physically, because he has bigger muscles? I find it interesting—and enlightening—to examine the true physiological differences between the sexes and to find how similar the two really are. I'd like very much to convince you that we are not the physically inferior gender, and that we have every right to develop our bodies along with our brothers instead of just cheering them on from the sideline.

In fact, some evidence implies that the female is in some ways the *stronger* sex. While 30 percent more males are conceived than females, only 6 percent more males are born, suggesting that a good percentage of males do not make it through the gestation period. At birth, life expectancy for males is sixty-six and two-thirds years; for females, it is seventy-four years. A recent study showed that 245 of 365 prevalent diseases occurred predominantly in males. And genetically, the female chromosome (XX) carries more enzymes and antibodies than does the male (XY), which is perhaps why females are less susceptible to disease.

It is true, of course, that males and females develop differently and at different rates. At puberty, the female undergoes radical changes due to her production of hormones, changes that include a widening of the pelvis, development of breasts, increased fat distribution around hips and thighs, growth of pubic hair and a dramatic end to the lengthening of her long bones. Bones ossify and, therefore, girls reach their adult height by sixteen plus or minus two years. Boys reach their adult height a bit later, by age eighteen plus or minus two years. The testes produce male hormones (androgens) that result in the male's sexual characteristics. (Females produce androgens too, though in smaller amounts, just as males produce tiny amounts of the female hormone, estrogen.) These extra years of growth result in the average male's greater size. By the time they both reach sixteen, chances are he will be taller, have a larger heart and other internal organs. His bones will be denser and his blood will contain more red cells and more oxygen-carrying hemoglobin. Finally, the male growth hormone, androgen, serves to stimulate the development of muscle tissue, which results in a greater ratio of muscle-to-fat than in females—and more muscle-to-fat makes for a more efficient physical machine.

Based on the above, it would seem that the male would be incontestably superior in strength and endurance. Not quite. Researchers today are suggesting that the gap between male and female physical potential—at least as it pertains to performance—is not as great as was once believed. Dr. Jack Wilmore of Arizona State University, for example, suggests that the quality of muscle, its contractile properties, its ability to exert force and its neuromuscular efficiency are the same in both sexes. In other words, if a man and a woman are of equal size and equal body-fat percentage, they will most likely be equally strong.

This is not to imply that women are soon about to surpass men in physical performance. While the female may be stronger relative to lean body weight, she must nevertheless perform with a higher fat percentage. The point, simply, is that studies such as Wilmore's show that the female is not as physically different from the male as many like to believe. And when one adds the fact that much of the female's so-called inferiority stems from various social and cultural obstacles, one begins to perceive the differences as even slighter. I have a friend who is working hard on her

body. Her husband is constantly coming out with remarks such as, "It's such a shame, honey, that you do all this work to develop your arms while I do absolutely nothing and you're still ten times smaller than I am." He not only undermines his wife's achievement of firm flesh but he misses the whole point of her individual potential. Her body-fat percentage is ideal, her heart and lungs are at peak efficiency from running every day, her muscles are beautifully toned from head to toe, and she feels ecstatic to be in such great shape. Her husband has let his hips spread slightly, has allowed a small roll to develop at his waist, and he runs once every two weeks—yet he considers *his* body superior to his wife's because his muscles are bigger. Big muscles do nothing for the quality of his life because he does nothing with them.

Should I say to this man: "It's such a shame that your resting pulse is thirty beats higher than mine. Don't even bother improving yours because you could never achieve the cardiovascular level with which I am gifted."? Of course not. He should get his resting pulse as low as possible for *himself*, not to compare it to mine.

Some exercise physiologists feel that with equal opportunity and activity, the gap between the sexes in physical performance could be closed to 10 percent or less. As a matter of fact, in East Germany, where coaching and encouragement are offered to girls from an early age, the gap has already narrowed remarkably. In half of the events at the Montreal Olympics in 1976, the East German women swimmers' performances measured up to at least 96 percent of the male standards.

Another researcher who is digging out positive information about the physical potential of women is Dr. Joan Ullyot, a marathon runner from San Francisco. Her theory is that women will prove to be superior at true endurance events after sociological inequalities are eliminated. She suggests that in events of near maximal effort lasting more than two hours, the male is incapable of utilizing his own stored energy and must ingest other energy sources to continue on. Such ingestion is often difficult for the body to negotiate at near maximal effort. Dr. Ullyot indicates that the female is more capable of converting her stored fat and using it for mechanical energy. As a female marathon swimmer who has competed against men for the last decade, I am intrigued by Dr. Ullyot's theory. I am the best example: I hold the record for the longest swim in history (89 miles) by either a male or a female.

Women, thus, *may be better* at long endurance events. They may be more resistant to disease. But yes, men tend to be bigger and stronger and faster. These facts *do not* mean that one sex is physically superior to the other.

Why Stimulate Muscle Growth?

But let's get down to the matter of *muscles*. Women are generally *not capable* of developing large, defined muscle groups—certainly not when compared to men. This is due to a shortage of testosterone (the male sex hormone) in the female system. And even those few women who can develop considerable size don't readily show it: Extra fatty tissue tends to hide pronounced muscle definition.

Resistance training is based on a methodical straining of the body's major muscle groups. The most common form of resistance training is weight lifting—an activity in which an isolated muscle group raises and lowers a weight until that muscle group is too fatigued to lift the weight one more time, thus stimulating the development of that muscle group.

Why stimulate muscle growth? First of all, the skeletal muscles, like the rest of the body, atrophy when not used. Muscle tissue shrinks and grows incapable of performing during exertion or stress. When the muscle tissue is stimulated it gains in endurance and allows you to do more with less fatigue. Strengthening the skeletal muscles also strengthens the bones themselves, as well as the ligaments, the tendons, the joints and connective tissue. Serious or even minor injuries from sports, unforeseen falls or any accidents, are far less prevalent in individuals who perform resistance exercises. Billie Jean King, after a number of knee operations, has often said that if she were to start her career over again, the one thing she would do differently would be to start lifting weights at the be-

ginning and continue on a weight training program throughout her life. She is convinced that her knees would have held up had she strengthened them throughout the years.

Resistance exercise will also help to lower body-fat percentage. Aerobic work does this by burning calories; resistance work does it in another way. Muscular growth is a complex phenomenon. In simplified terms, this is what happens: An intense muscular contraction (against resistance) causes the formation of a chemical called *creatine*. Creatine is the substance that induces RNA (ribonucleic acid) to stimulate muscle growth. *Myosin*, a protein, is formed, enabling the muscle to undergo additional contractions. Additional contractions produce creatine, which induces more growth. And so on. Remember that it is not technically the amount of fat that is important, but rather the percent of fat. In this case, the amount of fat remains constant with proper food intake and aerobic work while the amount of muscle increases with stimulation from resistance work. When this happens, the body-fat *percentage* becomes lower.

Muscular growth can even be of aerobic benefit. The process of muscular stimulation, although not an aerobic activity in itself (it is unlikely that the pulse could be maintained upward of 140 beats per minute for a continuous 15 minutes of resistance exercises—there would be some recovery time, however slight, in between exercises) it does produce minor aerobic results. For example, when I set out to do 50 push-ups, my pectorals (chest muscles) and biceps (front of the upper arms) must perform continuous and taxing work. By perhaps the thirtieth push-up, fatigue sets in and my heart works harder and harder to supply the pectorals and the biceps with the oxygen they need to complete 50. These skeletal muscles are forcing my heart to pump a greater volume of blood. When performing strenuous, continuous work like this, skeletal muscles are sometimes called auxiliary hearts. As the biceps, for example, become more and more desperate for fuel (oxygen and glycogen), they squeeze the blood more and more forcefully back to the heart for purification. The heart in turn responds forcefully to quickly get new fuel back to the biceps. So this demand on a large muscle

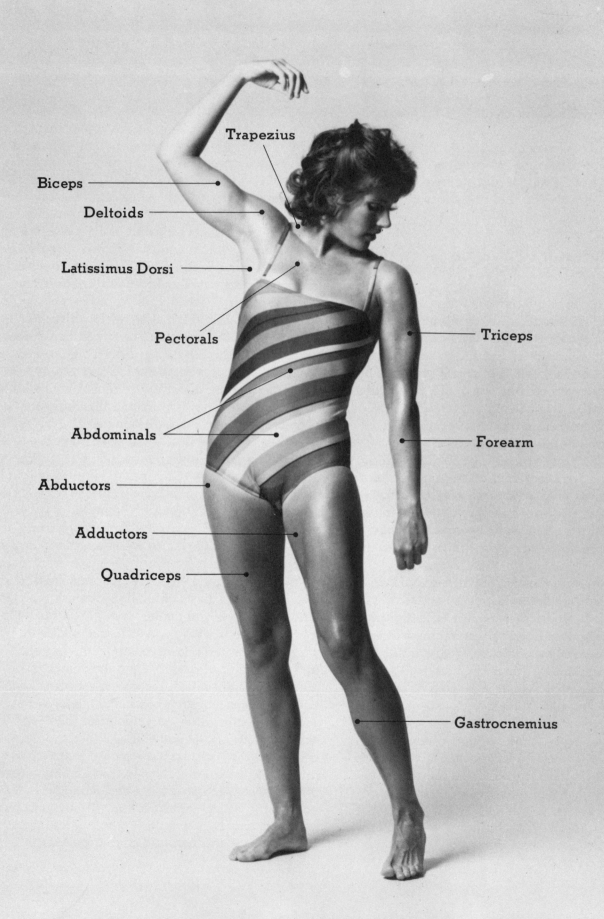

Biceps

Trapezius

Deltoids

Latissimus Dorsi

Pectorals

Triceps

Abdominals

Forearm

Abductors

Adductors

Quadriceps

Gastrocnemius

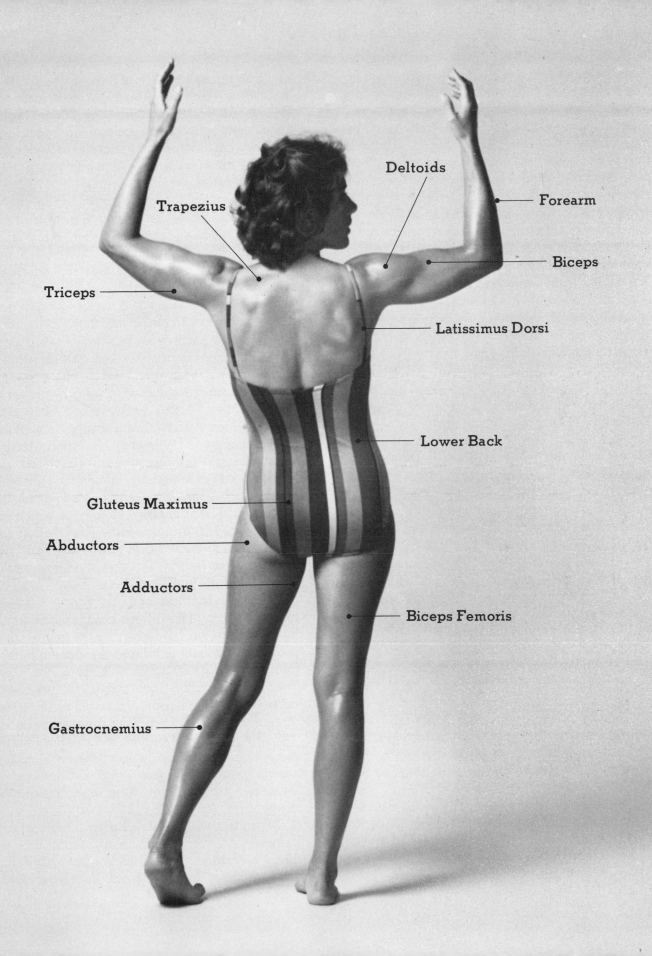

Deltoids

Forearm

Trapezius

Biceps

Triceps

Latissimus Dorsi

Lower Back

Gluteus Maximus

Abductors

Adductors

Biceps Femoris

Gastrocnemius

group actually helps the heart develop.

Most sports put some (but less than optimal) resistance on some of the large muscle groups. Racquet sports put continuous resistance on the quadriceps (the front of the thighs), the gluteus maximus (the buttocks) and one forearm; boxing puts great resistance on the deltoids (the shoulders); skiing and cycling put heavy resistance on the quadriceps. Other sports, such as swimming and rowing—if good technique is developed—put continuous and intense resistance on almost all the skeletal muscles. It is arguable, then, that these few sports could serve both as good aerobic workouts and resistance workouts. But to use swimming or rowing as a full-fledged resistance workout, you must participate at an almost expert level and with a supremely high degree of intensity. Most of us are not capable of this kind of energy, day after day. As a result, we must participate in resistance exercises specifically designed to stress the muscle groups of the body in a short period of time.

The human body has more than 434 skeletal muscles responsible for movement, but the following are the basic groups on which you'll want to concentrate resistance work. If you can successfully stimulate growth in these large groups, other minor groups will be affected in the process.

1. The lower back
2. Latissimus dorsi (the large fanlike muscles that laterally cover most of the back)
3. Deltoids (shoulder muscles)
4. Pectorals (chest muscles)
5. Trapezius (between the deltoids and the neck)
6. Triceps (back of the upper arm)
7. Biceps (the front of the upper arm)
8. Forearm (both sides of the forearm)
9. Quadriceps (front of the thigh)
10. Biceps femoris (back of the thigh or the hamstrings)
11. Gluteus maximus (the buttocks muscles)
12. Adductors (inside of the thigh)
13. Abductors (outside of the thigh)
14. Gastrocnemius (the calf muscles)
15. Abdominals (front and sides of the trunk)

Again, remember that if these basic fifteen groups are given a thorough workout, most of the 434 skeletal muscles will benefit. For example, if the biceps are worked hard enough by curling a bar from the outstretched palm up to under the chin, the muscles of the hands and wrists will be exercised adequately.

The types of resistance work available to you are (1) *isotonic* exercise, in which force is applied against a constant movable object—such as barbells or dumbbells, or more elaborate systems, such as a Universal gym; (2) *isometric* exercise in which force is exerted against an immovable object—such as pressing on a wall; (3) *accommodating resistance* exercise, in which the resistance changes along with your position of leverage during an isotonic contraction—such as Nautilus machines you strap yourself into, to work a specific muscle group. The amount of weight you are using here becomes heavier during the contraction because you are assuming a better position of leverage during the contraction; (4) *isokinetic* exercise, in which the speed of contraction is fixed and a maximum amount of resistance is met throughout the contraction by trying to complete the contraction quickly; and (5) *infimetric* exercise, in which one limb actually struggles against the other—such as on a pulley where the right arm tries to pull against the resistance that the left arm is offering at the other end of the cord.

Any one of these methods works. The object is to isolate each of the fifteen basic muscle groups, one at a time, and to resist enough force with each group until a level of fatigue is reached, making another contraction impossible. Thus, for Basic Training, it would be best for you to find a set of barbells and dumbbells, Universal or Nautilus equipment at your local Y, health spa or school facility. Or you should purchase a set of dumbbells to use at home. (Detailed instructions for all fifteen muscle groups using free weights, Universal and Nautilus equipment are found in the Weight Training Manual, pp. 91–125.)

Perhaps because women, as a general rule, have had little experience with weights or weight-lifting programs, it might be helpful to introduce you to some of the basic rules. No matter what equipment you use, try to copy the form in the photos that accompany the Weight Training Manual.

There are six cardinal rules for working with weights, regardless of which type of equipment you choose.

RULE 1: The Amount of Weight You Lift Is Not Important

It makes no difference whatsoever if you can lift 10 pounds or 100 pounds, as long as the weight provides the desired intensity for you. Ideally, you are attempting to achieve a certain weight for each muscle group, a weight that each muscle group should be able to raise and lower—with increasing difficulty—12 times. No more, no less.

If you have never worked with weights, you will not know, when you enter the weight room the first time, how much weight to use for any of the muscle groups. You will have to experiment for yourself; what someone else can lift has nothing to do with you. And, for that matter, what *your shoulders* can press (push) has nothing to do with what *your chest* can press. You might put 90 pounds on the bench press bar (to exercise the pectoral or chest muscles) and find that you cannot budge it; obviously that's too much weight. If you move the weight down to 60 pounds you might find you can just struggle through raising and lowering the bar 4 times—still too much weight because you cannot reach that magic number of 12. You move the weight down to 35 pounds and discover that you can easily do 20 repetitions (one repetition is one full cycle of raising and lowering the weight). Obviously, this weight is too light. But you now know that your ideal weight for the bench press, at least for the first couple of weeks until you get stronger, is somewhere between 35 and 60 pounds. You probably won't have to experiment much further to find the weight that you can press 12 times and only 12 times.

Let's say that directly after the bench press, you move to the military press (to exercise the deltoids, or shoulder muscles). The ideal weight for

you at this station will probably be less than it was at the bench press. Again, experiment to find the weight that you can press 12 times and only 12. And so on for each of the basic muscle groups. As a general rule, you will probably be able to handle more weight with the lower body than with the upper. The lower back and abdominal muscles are exercised by working against gravity instead of by moving a weight so some of the cardinal rules of weight lifting such as the ideal 12 repetitions will not apply to these two muscle groups—you should simply do the exercises shown in the Weight Training Manual until local failure (absolute fatigue) of the lower back or stomach muscles occurs, regardless of the number of repetitions.

RULE 2: Intensity Means Progress

Many women who know how to push themselves on the track, or in the pool, do not push themselves in the weight room. This is understandable given their inexperience with weights. It is common to see a strong young woman holding a 5-pound dumbbell in each hand, going through the motions of exercise with no strain whatsoever. Simply going through the motions in the weight room, without exertion, is as meaningless as going through the motions of your morning run. *Without intensity you cannot improve, you cannot progress.*

If you can perform 50 repetitions of a given contraction, let's say a bicep curl (curling a bar with arms outstretched down by your sides, elbows locked, to up under your chin), then that amount of resistance is far too easy. You will not stimulate the muscle to grow. If you can only perform two repetitions of a certain contraction, you help the explosiveness of that muscle group but you will be doing nothing for muscular endurance.

So that you will know what sort of intensity to expect, let's go through a set of 12 bench presses together. (See the photograph on p. 105 for form.)

You are lying, back down, on the bench. Your feet are up on the bench to protect your back, about 4 feet apart. Your hands are gripping the bar at shoulder width and the bar is 1 inch from your chest. In deep concentration, you focus your eyes on a point on the ceiling and you block out all sounds and voices in the room. All you can hear is your breath. You breathe in deeply, you secure your grip on the bar and as you begin to exhale, you press the bar slowly and smoothly toward the ceiling. You reach the point where your elbows lock, you pause for 1 full second and, as you begin to inhale, you slowly and smoothly lower the bar back down to within 1 inch of your chest. You have just completed 1 repetition—there are 11 to go.

The first rep felt slightly heavy as that muscle group has not been thoroughly warmed up. The second rep, performed with the same speed and control as the first, is a bit easier. The third, fourth and fifth reps are a snap. The sixth seems to get a little harder, as if someone had added just a couple of pounds when you weren't looking. The seventh and eighth are still within your control but your arms are feeling heavy now and you're thinking that you'll never get to 12. Before beginning the ninth rep, you shut your eyes in concentration and exhale forcefully as you squeeze it up. During the tenth rep, your arms will start to tremble; you will feel as though 1,000 pounds are right above your chest. The eleventh rep may not be smooth. Your strength is fading; you might pause halfway up. Grab another breath of air and push with your will as you exhale forcefully (almost as if you're pushing with your breath) until you reach the top. Your pectoral muscles will be spent after the eleventh rep. They will be burning and quivering, giving you the sign that they have had enough. This is the point where you reach for one more. With willpower you can squeeze the twelfth one out, beyond present exhaustion toward physical potential. You might want to have someone nearby lend you a supportive finger, literally, during that last supreme effort. Do this for every muscle group and you will truly come to know the benefits of a resistance workout. And don't forget: As your strength improves at each station, you will have to increase the weight accordingly so that you are always fighting for that twelfth rep.

RULE 3: Pay Strict Attention to Form

Try to imitate the form illustrated in the Weight Training Manual for the specific type of equipment you use. Aside from positioning yourself at the correct angle to the weight, and moving the weight at the correct angle away from you, always move the weight slowly and smoothly. This will help to isolate the muscle group you are working. If you jerk the weight around quickly, you are liable to use adjacent muscle groups to help you lift it. Second, if you squeeze the weight slowly up and then slowly down, the muscle group will be working hard at every point of the contraction instead of throwing the weight where momentum will make it easier at certain points of the contraction. In all cases, you should be very careful and precise during resistance work. Form is at least as important, if not more so, than the amount of weight being used.

Don't be afraid to ask an instructor or a competent friend exactly how to perform each resistance exercise if you don't have your copy of *Basic Training* with you at the weight room. *Form means everything.* Weights should not be jerked or banged or thrown. Control through the proper angle and range of movement will produce the best results for both strength and flexibility.

RULE 4: Variety Is Important

As in aerobic exercise, you cannot do the same workout every time for months and months—the muscles will eventually fail to respond. Increase the amount of weight as you achieve the 12 reps, reduce the amount of rest between stations, throw in an occasional "negative" set of 12 repetitions. "Negative" repetitions are eccentric contractions (or the lowering part of a normal repetition) where the muscle is lengthening throughout the repetition.

For example, you are handed the barbell with your arms fully extended toward the ceiling; then on your own you lower the bar down to your chest, at which point your trainer raises it to the extended position again. The weight on the bar is far too much for you to push up but just enough for you to lower 12 times. Many studies show that "negatives" result in great increases of strength in a short amount of time.

When we say that weight training will stimulate muscle growth, you may wonder why there is not continual growth going on until you reach the size of Arnold Schwarzenegger! "Why, if I push each muscle group to the limit twice a week, stimulating each muscle group to grow twice a week, won't I get bigger and bigger and bigger?" First of all, earlier in this chapter you have read about the hormonal limitations of developing past a certain size. Each individual has a certain potential for muscle tone, muscle size and muscular definition; Basic Training, with its cardinal rules of weight training, aims toward helping each person reach her particular potential. And if you follow these rules faithfully you will witness *your own* tone, size and definition develop before your very eyes. Once you reach your potential, however, all the work you do twice a week is to *maintain* that potential—to keep atrophy and flaccidness of muscle tissue from recurring. At this point in your conditioning, variety can be very helpful because your muscles may be so accustomed to the same old routine that even maintaining that level will be difficult if the routine is not varied somewhat.

I encouraged my literary agent to start on a Nautilus routine two years ago and she went at it like a mad hatter, faithfully showing up twice a week and always working very hard. And her hard work showed. She toned beautifully, and she also became incredibly strong. Inevitably, she reached a point of peak strength and now can no longer vary her workout by increasing the amount of weight she uses. She will have to become creative and learn how to use negatives, chin-ups, varied push-ups, etc., to keep her mind and her muscles interested in the weight room. I have offered several of these creative variations in Advanced Training (see pp. 127–155).

RULE 5: Rest Must Be Respected

Rest between workouts is more important in resistance than in aerobic training. In aerobic training, the conditioned heart will recover very quickly after a workout. But even well-trained muscles are filled with waste products after an intense workout.

Resistance work is done at the same frequency by all athletes of Basic Training: twice a week, preferably on the second and fifth days. The days in between give the tired tissue 72 hours or more to repair itself (48 hours rest will be sufficient if you want to work every other day—twice a week is the minimum for Basic Training). An intense workout with weights usually causes breakdown of the tissue that has been pushed to exhaustion. (This breakdown does not happen as much during aerobic workouts because, although you are pushing muscles, you are never pushing to absolute exhaustion—after all, *continuous* activity is the point of aerobics.) This breakdown is a necessary first step toward muscle growth; nevertheless, time is needed for the muscle to recuperate fully before being torn down again. Otherwise, fatigue sets in and the muscle may eventually collapse under severe injury.

This comfortable spread between resistance sessions allows the body to flush out certain waste products that have gathered in the tired muscles (lactic acid, which promotes fatigue and soreness) and replenish the nutrients that have been lost during the exhaustion process (especially potassium). These processes can take at least 48 hours. I have found that two workouts a week, at maximal effort, is the optimal number of workouts, although you may be able to handle three a week. Don't sacrifice intensity for frequency, however.

RULE 6: Don't Forget to Breathe

During moments of intense effort with weights, a common mistake is to hold one's breath, waiting to breathe when the effort subsides. Don't do this. You must breathe *continuously* while lifting weights, just as if you were playing a sport or performing an aerobic activity. If you don't breathe you put a dramatic strain on the heart, which is trying to supply oxygen to that muscle group you are exercising. Also, you will find that exhaling while you press (lift) on the weight and inhaling while you release (lower) it, is the most effective breathing pattern to get you through the 12 reps.

No matter which type of weight-lifting equipment you use, follow these rules. There are plenty of tricks to lifting weights without exerting much effort, such as using nearby muscles for increased leverage or throwing the weight with some velocity to gain momentum. You have no one to fool in Basic Training but yourself. Don't be self-conscious when you enter the weight room; your muscles are the same in quality as everyone else's, male or female, regardless of the amount of weight you are capable of moving. Have the guts to put the ideal weight on the bar for yourself at each station—and keep up the willpower to push through to the twelfth rep.

PART II
BASIC TRAINING

CHAPTER 4

Are You Ready to Begin?

The six-day-a-week routine of Basic Training is not arbitrary. The ratio of stretching to 90/90's to weights to aerobics is not arbitrary. The full rest day a week is not arbitrary.

Basic Training incorporates the most recent research on female conditioning and takes into account the personal experiences of finely tuned women athletes. I have given the program to a wide range of friends with varying backgrounds: to those who have virtually *never* engaged in physically vigorous activity; to women over sixty; to women with histories of smoking, overeating, alcoholism, drug use; to women who were in pretty good shape to begin with. I have seen Basic Training work for all of them, that is, all who were willing to stick to the schedule.

Following the schedule is crucial. You must make more than a passing commitment. Occasional jogging is not enough; a weekly trip to a fitness club is not enough; a yearly trip to a health spa is not enough; weekend tennis is not enough; 10 minutes of calisthenics a day is not enough. While Basic Training does not demand an unreasonable amount of your time, it does require daily participation.

Basic Training is not designed as a short-term weight-loss program; but you should become slimmer gradually and effectively. Nor is it designed to lower your blood pressure before your next doctor's appointment; it is meant to ease work for your heart and lungs over your lifetime. The trick to the success of Basic Training is for you to think of it as a

natural, necessary, enjoyable part of your daily life. Even when not training for a specific sport, I will always have—for the rest of my life—a daily exercise routine to look forward to. I would no sooner abandon my program for burning fat and stimulating my heart and skeletal muscles than I would abandon brushing my teeth.

Although the concepts and actual exercises are of benefit to a wide variety of people (including men), Basic Training is specially designed for a certain group of women. Some of you have a mild interest in getting your bodies in a little better shape. Some of you have more than a mild interest but are not sufficiently confident of your present physical state. You know that you have been inactive for too long, that you have been eating the wrong foods. You would like to feel better, look better, and are willing to do *something*. But you may take a glimpse at Basic Training and make tracks in the opposite direction—the thought of exercising *six days a week*, when perhaps you have only exercised strenuously six times a year, might be terrifying. The thought of lifting weights is beyond your imagination. Well, don't go away. More than for anyone else, Basic Training is for you.

Indeed, for those of you who focus relatively little on the physical, but who show a flicker of desire to improve your bodies, Basic Training is the answer. You may not be able to *always* play by the rules—frequent, intense and precise participation. You may quit now and then before you finish. You may, at times, abandon regular activity for the sake of your job, family or social occasions. Even so, you can still, by *almost* always playing by the rules, lower your resting pulse and body-fat percentage and feel pride in your physical capabilities. If you read through Basic Training and come to understand its concepts and principles, the few minutes you spend cycling, swimming or lifting weights will pay off. *Don't shy away from Basic Training just because you feel you are not prepared.* As a matter of fact, a month of "warm-up" exercises has been offered with you in mind.

If you have not exercised strenuously for several years, if you have *never* exercised strenuously, if you are 25 pounds or more overweight, if you have recently overused tobacco, alcohol, or drugs, if you have some serious medical history that worries you, if you are over forty, take the following three precautions:

1. get a checkup and a go-ahead from a physician;
2. follow, to the letter, the month of "warm-up" before Basic Training;
3. repeat the month of "warm-up" for a second month if you could not do it extremely easily the first time around.

After a go-ahead from a doctor and one or two months of "warm-up," you will be ready to begin.

Don't Underestimate Yourself

Many women today are extremely motivated and aggressive and have no problems leaping right into Basic Training on day one. But even an unselfconscious, confident woman has a definite tendency to underestimate herself when it comes to physical tests. Recently I was at a photography shooting with four women from *Redbook* magazine, all in their thirties, all full of gusto and all into their first month of Basic Training. When I arrived, one of them confessed that she couldn't possibly do a 90/90 (see p. 78) for more than 15 seconds, that she had been trying her best every day but she collapsed after 12 seconds. I leaned her against the wall, she lowered herself into position, and I timed her and coached her through a full minute, which she handled easily. Then halfway through the photo session in which a small, thin model was posing with 10-pound dumbbells, another woman from *Redbook* said to me: "You know, I use two-and-one-half-pound dumbbells at home for all my Basic Training exercises. Why can the model who is smaller than I use so much more weight?" I had her go through a few sets of her exercises with the 10-pound weights, which she handled like feathers. She needed even heavier weights to do her any good; yet she chose ridiculously light weights that would be appropriate for a seven-year-old to use at home. Just as you should take precautions to start slowly if you feel you're not ready for Basic Training, *do not underestimate yourself* once you are ready. Listen carefully to the language I have used in describing to you how you should feel after your 15 minutes on the stationary bike and after your twelfth bench press. Don't cheat yourself by underachieving.

Your Fitness Rating

Whether you begin with the month of Warm-up or Basic Training itself, or move right to the Advanced Training Manual, try to evaluate precisely your initial fitness level first. Precision of measurement will help you evaluate your fitness progress. Of course, if you feel fantastic and you look toned after two months of Basic Training, the program is obviously working for you. But after all, Basic Training is designed to improve the efficiency of the cardiovascular and muscular systems and these improvements can and should be measured instead of just being judged by your emotional state and approval of your reflection in the mirror.

Check yourself on the following evaluations, regardless of your current fitness status, the day before you begin Basic Training. Check yourself again at your six-month mark and every six months thereafter. A few of the tests, such as body-fat percentage, will be difficult for you to perform by yourself. Do your best to have them performed by your doctor, university health or sports medicine department, or a local health club or Y before you begin the program. Then have these difficult tests done once a year, doing the easier tests yourself every six months. (Many health spas that perform these tests as a service for their members will often, for a nominal fee, test nonmembers.) If there are a few evaluations you simply cannot manage to have tested by an expert, do as many of the tests that you can perform yourself. Record and date all the results of these evaluations so that you can check your progress accurately.

1. Resting Pulse Rate

Take your pulse for a minute upon waking, before getting out of bed. Your resting pulse should steadily drop at six-month intervals if you're beginning Basic Training as a stranger to regular exercise. Your resting pulse should be taken for a full 60 seconds for accuracy. (During aerobic activity to ensure that no recovery has begun, take your pulse for only 6 seconds and multiply by ten.)

2. Pulse Recovery Rate

Run (a treadmill will do) or cycle (a stationary ergometer will do) for 12 continuous minutes at the most intense pace possible for you. Take your pulse immediately upon finishing. (It should be higher than 80 percent of 220 minus your age.) Then take your pulse once a minute after finishing the intense exercise until it drops under 90. The day before you begin Basic Training, it may take 25 minutes for your pulse to drop under 90. After six months, it may take only 10 minutes to drop. And so on.

    25 minutes indicates a poor fitness level
    10 minutes is still a fairly long recovery time
     5 minutes indicates a decent recovery time
     3 minutes and under is excellent

Of course, many of you just beginning Basic Training will not be able to run 12 intense, continuous minutes. Run (or cycle) as many minutes as you possibly can and follow the recovery pulse procedure as described above. Then do the 12-minute test after your sixth month.

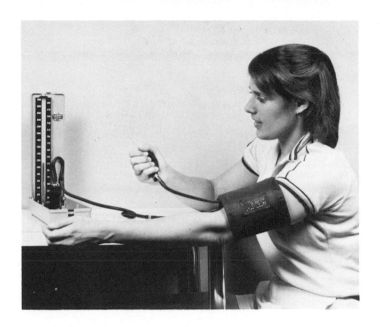

3. Blood Pressure

You will probably have to get someone to check this for you. More and more studies link high blood pressure with most forms of coronary heart disease. Basic Training should lower your blood pressure. The optimum blood pressure varies for different age categories and different-sized individuals. These days physicians generally agree that 140/90 is the maximum acceptable blood pressure. The qualified person who checks your blood pressure will tell you whether you would be better off with a lower reading.

4. Body-Fat Percentage

You will have to get an expert to measure this for you. Most people do a skin-fold calibration. Women in the U.S. today average from 22 to 26 percent body fat. This is simply too high. You should shoot for a body-fat percentage of under 18 percent. Basic Training is designed to lower body-fat percentage; every six months, your body-fat percentage should decrease. A small population of women athletes register less than 10 percent body fat. You don't need to be that low to be fit and healthy. As a gen-

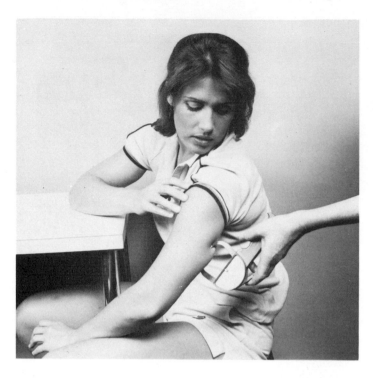

eral rule, you will be doing your heart—not to mention your appearance—a big favor if you are less than 18 percent body fat. Eighteen percent might sound easy to you but, believe me, it will take consistent hard work to dip under this percent.

5. Muscular Strength

The standard tests for muscular strength are the number of (a) bent-leg sit-ups; (b) full push-ups; (c) chin-ups you can do. Chin-ups are particularly difficult for women because they are a test of your arm strength relative to your body weight; women have such comparatively weak upper body strength with such a low center of gravity that chin-ups present a whopping challenge. Even if you cannot do one chin-up before Basic Training, you may be able to do one or two after six months. And your numbers of bent-leg sit-ups and full push-ups will increase considerably. So many women think they can't do a full, regular push-up because they were always told they could only do them from their knees. Concentrate and put all your effort into the regular kind. You'll get it, even if it's just one at a time.

6. Flexibility

There are many tests for flexibility. The easiest ones in this case are to attempt to imitate, precisely, the stretching exercises illustrated on pages 67–77. If you are literally a yard away from touching the points indicated, don't give up. Like muscular strength, flexibility can be improved. After six months of Basic Training, your flexibility will increase tremendously.

7. Body Measurements

Record your waist, hips, each thigh, chest and each upper arm measurement before beginning Basic Training. There is no accounting for taste—some people like very thin arms and a tiny waist. Basic Training should increase the size of your arms, chest, and waist, and decrease the size of your hips and thighs. You will have more solid muscle and better tone. Record these measurements every six months to see how the proportion of your body is changing. Your upper body measurements should increase while the lower body will decrease.

The Key to Improvement Is Precision

Fitness programs that prescribe exercising "until you feel great and until you know it is time to stop" are familiar to us all. We can appreciate the appealing simplicity. We also appreciate the fact that common sense should always play a role in athletic endeavors. Occasions will most certainly arise throughout your experience with Basic Training when common sense tells you to stop.

But beyond plain sense, we have found that the most effective Basic Training results from *carefully planned and timed activity*. Arbitrary attention to one segment of your workout frequently allows carelessness to pervade all segments. In the end, you may be rationalizing ways to ease and shorten all aspects of Basic Training. Thus, a basic rule in Basic Training is to perform what you set out to per-

Checklist before Starting

1. Always have a second hand in view on the wall, on your wrist or on a stopwatch.
2. Make sure your clothing is loose enough to allow free breathing and easy movement.
3. Wear a sports bra if you feel discomfort or are embarrassed by bouncing breasts. A sports bra can be much easier on the breasts, particularly during menstruation or lactation. There are many styles available. As a matter of fact, regardless of the time of the month, a good sports bra is a good idea. Not only will it be more comfortable for you and prevent inhibition of your enthusiasm, but also it will keep the mammary tissue and ligaments from stretching.
4. Don't eat a full meal for at least 3 hours before a workout.
5. Feel free to drink directly before and during your workout if you are thirsty but try to avoid the following:
   a. any carbonated beverages—you don't need carbon dioxide, you need oxygen
   b. coffee or tea—you don't need a jolt to the nervous system when adrenalin is already doing the job
   c. alcohol—you want to be alert, not duller
6. Don't stretch or do sit-ups/abdominal work on a hard floor—use a rug or mat.
7. Use a log book to record your daily workouts, the date of resting pulse readings, 6-month self-evaluations and great personal breakthroughs in workouts.
8. Keep your Basic Training goals in mind before you start each workout and keep them in focus if things get tough or if you get bored. Make yourself reach your goal; don't just continue according to how you feel—unless you feel a sharp pain that could signal an injury (not a "stitch").
9. Know the pulse rate you are shooting for during aerobic workouts (80% of 220 minus your age).
10. Make sure the weights you use are heavy enough to tax you for that twelfth rep. Know the amount of weight you are shooting for at each muscle group station.

form. If you are at the workout stage that prescribes 3 minutes of 90/90's, spend *3 full minutes.* If you are going to swim for 20 minutes, rest for 2, and swim another 10, your aerobic workout will be complete only after 32 minutes. Following the prescribed rest time at each workout is equally important.

Precise measurement is critical to Basic Training. Your measurement of each workout's length and intensity (e.g., your pulse) should be *exact.* By being precise, you may expect to achieve your fitness goals more quickly. You will find that Basic Training can be extremely enjoyable; you will also find that it will not succeed if you run whenever you feel like it, for whatever time you choose.

Taking Your Pulse

You should take your pulse first thing in the morning once a week, preferably on the day after your rest day. Use a good watch with a second hand and count the beats for one PRECISE minute—from either your wrist or your neck. For the first six months of Basic Training, record your weekly pulse for comparison's sake. It may rise moderately for the first two or three weeks, if your level of Basic Training is quite a step up from whatever you had been doing. But after six months of dedicated work, your resting pulse should be considerably lower than on the day you started.

How much your pulse decreases will depend upon several factors. If you started out in pretty good shape, say with a pulse of 65 (the national average for women is 72), then with three months' work you may only be able to get it down to 61, a considerable improvement when you remember that the initial pulse rate was so good. If you start with a pulse of 85, three months of precise daily Basic or Advanced Training could mean a drop of 15 beats per minute, or a pulse of 70. Of course, if

you have special problems of obesity and high blood pressure, lowering the resting pulse will not be as easy.

During stretching, you should look for a slight rise in your pulse—about 20 beats—which means circulation is stepping up slightly as the muscles are warming with the increase flow of blood. Always remember what minimum pulse to look for during aerobics: 80 percent of 220 minus your age.

During an intense weight workout your pulse should be fairly high, perhaps 10 or 15 beats under 80 percent of 220 minus your age. And you would expect this same weight workout pulse by the end of your 90/90's sessions.

There is one other time when pulse rate measurement might be useful. After the first six months of Basic Training, you might take your morning resting pulse in the middle of the week on the day after an especially strenuous workout. Don't worry if your pulse is 5 or 6 beats higher than what is normal for you at the time. The body is working to repair some of the fatigued tissue from yesterday's hard work. If your pulse is 10 beats higher than normal, however, it may be a signal that breakdown is extensive and the body needs recuperation. Common sense should tell you that a day off, or at least a very light day, is in order. During the first six months, this test is usually not applicable because your body has not grown accustomed to frequent strenuous exercise so don't worry if your resting pulse rate measurements seem erratic. After six months though, the pulse will have settled into a pattern and any major deviation will be an indication that something may be wrong.

Using a Stopwatch

A necessary tool in helping you develop precision during all aspects of Basic Training is a stopwatch or a second-hand sweep on your wristwatch. Your workouts are set in precise combinations of minutes—and they are impossible to carry out without constant reference to a second-hand sweep. There are many inexpensive and sturdy stopwatches available these days, both hand-held and wrist models. Many good wristwatches with second hands are sturdy enough to be worn during strenuous exercise.

Have your watch with you at all times. (Swimming may pose difficulties, but there are diving watches that are lightweight enough to wear in the pool. Some pool areas have large wall clocks with second hands. Or ask the lifeguard to whistle to you after a specific time.)

Refer to your watch at all stages of your workout. Stretch for the designated time. (Additional stretching will not hurt.) Time yourself to the second during aerobic workouts. Be aware of how long your intense weight workouts are taking you. Gabbing or daydreaming between stations undermines your progress. Use your watch occasionally to check your pulse during all phases of Basic and Advanced Training—but *especially* during aerobics where pulse rate means everything.

Changes to Look for after Six Months of Basic Training

Outer Changes

1. Wider shoulders
   - The skeleton won't widen but the deltoids will flesh out and give a slightly broader appearance
2. More slender hips
   - There is very little muscle on the hips so by shedding your excess fat, the hip bones themselves will reveal their line; also, your hips will appear narrower in contrast to your new wider shoulders
3. Higher and firmer breasts
   - The breasts themselves will not grow but the stronger pectoral muscles will lift them
4. Better bone structure in the face
   - Your lower body-fat percentage and overall muscle tone will also show in your face, pulling your skin tauter to make your eyes look larger and to sculpt your cheekbone and jaw lines
5. Flatter stomach
   - All of the torso, the sides, and the upper and lower stomach, will be taut from the attention given to abdominals during weight training
6. Higher and firmer buttocks
   - You will lose fat and develop muscle in the buttocks; the muscle will draw the buttocks higher and a tight contour will replace the vague sag of earlier days
7. Shapelier upper arms
   - With all the bicep and tricep work twice a week at weight training, fleshy upper arms will tone down and follow shapely curves; skinny or bony upper arms will fill out
8. More slender thighs
   - The measurement of the thighs will be the most dramatic reduction in the first six months of Basic Training; loss of fat through aerobics and leg strengthening through 90/90's and weights will allow both the outer and the inner thigh to become firmer
9. Face and body skin clearer
   - The daily cycle of producing heavy sweat and then replenishing the fluids by drinking healthy amounts of water and fruit juice will clean the pores of the skin
10. Shapelier calves
    - All six of the aerobic exercises will develop calf muscles and give them a curved but not bulky shape; and the weight work will sculpt the outside edges of the calves
11. Clearer eyes and sweeter breath and body odor
    - As your heart and lungs become more efficient and your body-fat percentage lowers, all of your systems function with less effort and less resistance—excess mucous is removed from the system, making breathing easier and your eyes clearer without the mucous film; excess toxins are removed from the system, making your breath and body odor sweeter

Inner Changes

1. More energy
   - Regular, strenuous aerobics will produce and stimulate all your systems, giving you more energy; also, because your heart will have an easier job and your body will carry less of a fat burden, you will have more energy throughout your working hours
2. Tire less easily
   - The compound of daily activities that used to tire you will no longer faze you in the least: your new heart and lungs will allow you to run for a bus without breathing hard; your new legs will not weaken when you climb stairs or stand for

long periods; your new back will not ache when you sit for hours; and your new arms, shoulders and back will allow you to lift and carry your own suitcases with little effort

3. Resistance to some illnesses
   ● Your more efficient systems will develop a higher resistance to colds and flus

4. Better disposition
   ● Because of your higher energy level and higher self-esteem regarding your new strong and capable body, your disposition will follow a more even keel; you will handle pressure and stress better; you will flare up less at minor aggravations; you will not experience the previous lows and minor depressions as often

5. More positive attitude
   ● Your self-assurance and self-confidence will be constant because your body will be slimmer and

stronger; now that you are achieving workouts you never thought possible six months ago, other aspects of your life are also seen now in a more positive light and other goals become achievable

6. Sleep better
   ● Your higher energy will mean putting more intensity into your work, your relationships, your workouts; you will now go to sleep because you need to instead of out of habit; you will sleep deep quality hours and wake up excited to get going instead of distracted sleep when you wake up groggy and remain half-asleep for hours

7. Better diet
   ● The more sedentary you are, the more you crave heavy and fattening foods; if you are active and in shape, you will not only yen for fruits and salads and

light foods but your appetite will be appropriate for what your body can use

8. Better sex
   ● Because your entire body will be operating more efficiently and more sensitively, all your senses will be more acute—your sight, hearing, touch, and sexual response will be keen

9. Easier menstrual cycles
   ● Your blood vessels will now be stronger and wider to allow easy blood flow and you will consequently experience fewer cramps and less general discomfort during your period

10. Less prone to injuries
    ● You will be more flexible from stretching and more sure-footed and in control of your body from aerobics and weight training so that twisted ankles and other injuries from sudden unexpected circumstances will be less likely

CHAPTER 5

Stretching Exercises and 90/90's

Now you're ready to spring into action! Let me teach you the full complement of stretching exercises, how to move through the set quickly and why you need to do the set twice a day. Let me coach you through a 90/90. It won't be easy and it will take you a while to build up to a full 90/90 but the results of the simple exercise will be noticeable in firmer thighs. I will show you the ins and outs of weights in the Weight Training Manual, which is the first chapter of the next section. Then you will choose an aerobic activity (or more than one) and start your first day of Basic Training.

Stretching

Stretching lengthens and warms muscle fibers before and after strenuous exercise. Stretching helps prevent possible injuries. If a cold, tight muscle is suddenly shocked into a violent contraction (for example, running fast with no warm-up), it may tear, pull or strain. Or injury may occur in the muscle fascia (the sheath covering the muscle), in a tendon, a ligament, the cartilage or even a bone in the form of a stress fracture. Lengthening and warming the muscle fibers allows them to be more flexible, so that they are prepared to accommodate any strain demanded of them once contractions (or exercises) begin.

Flexibility of the muscles and joints is desirable in any sport. It increases endurance; better form can generally be achieved. But don't worry if you

are "tight," or inflexible. Some of the greatest athletes in the world are so tight they don't have a prayer of touching their toes. Your flexibility relative to others means nothing; you should only be concerned with becoming as flexible as you can— to improve your performance and your comfort while working out. The greatest gains in flexibility come with stretching when the muscles are very warm, directly after strenuous exercise. It is then that the muscle can really lengthen without risk of injury; you can push it a little bit because it is warm and willing to be shaped. Stretching is necessary before and after your workouts. Each session should be conscientiously conducted.

You must stretch during Basic Training, regardless of your exercise schedule and your particular stage of fitness (and as I've outlined in the Warm-up Month). In conjunction with your aerobic workout, you should perform ALL the stretching exercises once before aerobics and then again perform ALL of them after aerobics. If you move efficiently through the list, spending only 15 seconds on each position and fluidly switching to the next position you will complete the list in precisely 5 minutes. Most people's concept of proper stretching is a long session in a semitrance. Spending only 15 seconds in each position and quickly switching to the next position will initially seem very rushed to you. The key is correct form. If you can imitate the full stretched position of the photos, 15 seconds at each position before AND after aerobics will help your training progress immeasurably. You will find yourself more able to give 100 percent intensity to the workout if you STRETCH.

The time prescribed for stretching in Basic Training and at each level of Advanced Training is the *minimum* for that level of aerobic work. You may put in more time on days when you are particularly stiff *and* you may add other stretching exercises to those offered here. Note that here in Basic Training you spend 15 seconds at each station twice—whereas you spent one 30-second session at each station in the warm-up month.

There are nine basic stretching positions, each designed to lengthen and warm a major muscle group. Each of the nine has one or more specific stretches listed under it. You are to give 15 seconds to each specific stretch. Certain general techniques apply to each of them.

1. When stretching, always relax your entire body.
2. Assume your stretched position (imitate the form pictured as closely as possible) for approximately 15 seconds. If a muscle group is particularly tight, repeat for 15 seconds. *Do not bounce;* always stretch in one slow, relaxed movement.
3. Move on to the next position. If 5 minutes of stretching are suggested before your Monday's aerobic workout, for example, move quickly through the basic stretching exercises, spending approximately 15 seconds at each position. If you want to spend 10 minutes stretching, you may spend 30 seconds at each position or longer at certain tight muscle groups.
4. Do not stretch on a hard floor; use a rug or mat.
5. Do not hurt yourself by forcing a position you're not yet ready for. On the other hand, don't limit yourself by the photos. I am not limber like a dancer and you may be able to stretch farther than I. Go for it!

You should be able to see improvement with each passing week. On the first day you may only be able to touch your ankles while reaching to touch your toes; six weeks later you may extend your hands around your sneakers with your nose touching your knees. And you will also see improvement in your aerobic and weight workouts. The pre-stretch will warm the muscles and allow you to work hard right at the start of the workout. And the stretching session after workouts will help get the kinks out and relieve excess soreness.

1. HAMSTRINGS (back of thigh) and ADDUCTORS (inside of thigh)

a. Sit on the floor with legs spread as far apart as possible, knees locked. Lean forward from the waist (try not to curve your back) reaching your hands out in front of you as far as possible. Keep your elbows locked so when you're leaning forward you're stretching your sides. (The farther apart the legs are spread, the more you're stretching the adductors.)

b. Same position; leaning from the waist again, simultaneously reach the right hand toward the right foot and the left hand toward the left foot. (If you can, without unlocking the knees, hold your feet with your hands.) Your elbows will have to bend for this one.

c. Same position; leaning from the waist, reach both hands toward the left foot. Try to touch your nose to your left knee, knee locked.

d. Same position; reach both hands toward your right foot.

Note: Remember, you're leaning from the waist, trying not to curve your back and you're keeping your knees locked. Try to touch your nose to your left knee and then to your right.

2. HAMSTRINGS (back of thigh)

Sit on the floor, legs together and stretched directly in front of you, knees locked and feet flexed so that the toes are pointing to the ceiling. Sit relaxed. Bend from the waist and try to touch your chest to your thighs—in this position, your nose will touch your knees. You can hook your hands anywhere around the feet, but try to grasp your toes.

Note: Remember, you're bending from the waist, trying not to curve your back, knees locked, feet flexed. Try to relax and don't forget to breathe.

3. HAMSTRINGS and LOWER BACK

"The Plow": Lie on your back on the floor, palms flat on the floor by your sides, knees bent. Then raise your legs over your head, knees locked and toes flexed, and slowly lower them behind you. Try to touch your toes to the floor behind your head.

Note: In the correct position, you're looking up between your knees toward the ceiling, and your toes are touching the floor in a flexed position.

4. GLUTEUS MAXIMUS (buttocks)

a. Lie flat on the floor on your back. Bring the right knee up and pull with your hands to hold it tight into your chest. The left leg must remain outstretched, KNEE LOCKED, in order for this stretch to work.

b. Then bring the left knee up, while returning the right to an outstretched position, knee locked. Hold the knee in tight by gripping it with your hands.

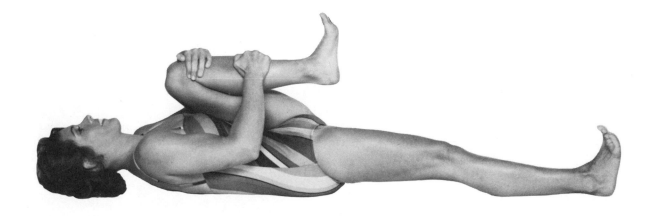

5. QUADRICEPS (front of thigh)

a. Stand up. Grab your right ankle behind you with both hands and pull it up toward your buttocks, while you point the knee to the floor. Look straight ahead.

b. Squat on the floor; put your hands behind you for support while you lean back. (The heels of the hands should be at the edge of the buttocks.) Now raise your pelvis toward the ceiling until your thighs are parallel to the floor. You should form one parallel line from your shoulders to your knees. (Raise the pelvis toward the ceiling by rising from the heels so that you end up on your toes.) Remember, don't move your hands or your feet from their starting spot on the floor.

c. Repeat (b) with the left leg.

6. QUADRICEPS and HAMSTRINGS

a. "Bicycles": Sit on the floor, stretch your right leg out in front of you and bend your left leg by pulling your left heel back toward your buttocks, the top of your left foot on the floor. Legs should be about 12 inches apart.
Lean back as far as you can go. Try to touch both shoulder blades to the floor while your buttocks and your left knee are touching the floor. If you can't get your shoulder blades to the floor at first, lean back as far as you can, propping yourself up on your elbows. This will still stretch the quads.

b. Same starting position. Bend forward from the waist over your extended leg and try to touch your knee with your nose. Try to hold the extended, flexed foot with your hands, and try not to curve your back.

c. Now extend your left leg out in front of you and pull your right heel back toward your buttocks. Lean back as in (a) above.

d. Bend forward over your left leg as in (b) above.

7. CALVES (back of the lower leg)

Stand 2½ feet from a wall, facing it, with your knees locked.

Keeping your heels flat on the floor, put your palms against the wall at chest height and lean in toward the wall. Hold that position for 15 seconds. The further you stand from the wall, the more difficult the stretch.

8. DELTOIDS (shoulders)

Stand with your knees slightly bent, arms loose by your sides, back straight.

a. Rotate the left arm backward from the shoulder 10 times.

b. Rotate the left arm forward 10 times.

c. Rotate the right arm backward 10 times.

d. Rotate the right arm forward 10 times.

e. Swing both arms simultaneously forward 10 times.

f. Swing both arms simultaneously backward 10 times.

Note: Rotate your arms in a wide circle and remember to keep your elbows locked and your hands relaxed.

9. UPPER SPINE and TORSO

a. "The Speed Skater": Stand with feet 12 inches apart, knees slightly bent and bend forward from the waist until your back is parallel to the floor. With the arms straight out to the sides from the shoulders, swing your arms from side to side by rotating the trunk at the waist.

b. "The Windmill": Keep your feet in the same position, knees slightly bent, standing straight up, arms out at shoulder height; swing your arms from front to back by rotating the trunk at the waist.

Note: Remember to keep your elbows locked for both exercises.

90/90's

The exercise I call 90/90's strengthens the quadriceps and firms the entire thigh. Buttocks and calves also benefit. Do 90/90's six days a week as part of Basic Training. Do them when you get up in the morning or right before you leave for work. Do them while you're watching television or during your lunch hour. Do them anytime, anywhere; just be sure to wear sneakers or shoes without heels. Be within sight of a watch or clock with a second hand because you must exactly time two 90-second periods. You will be shocked to discover the noticeable results of this convenient exercise after only a

few weeks. Your entire thigh will be remarkably firmer. Don't be discouraged if you can't do the full two periods right off. Few people can. Even my professional-athlete friends couldn't make the two periods right off. Build up to it as you started to do in the warm-up month. Start with 30 seconds, then 45, then a minute. Then go 2 periods of 45 seconds each with 15 seconds' rest in between. Eventually you will make it through to a full 90/90—90 seconds down in the first position, 30 seconds standing up resting, 90 seconds down in the second position. And if a full 90/90 ever becomes too easy for you,

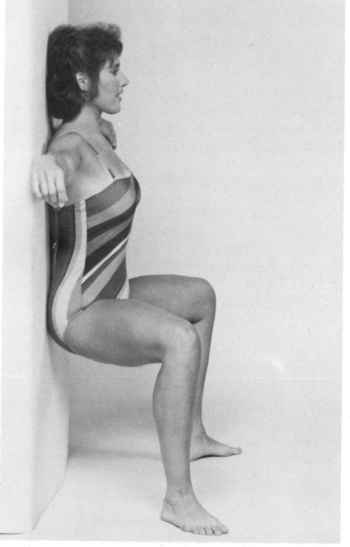

just tack on more time in both positions. I now spend 5 minutes down in the first position and then 5 minutes in the second, whereas a regular 90/90 used to be all I could handle.

● Stand with your back to a wall or a firm straight-backed vertical surface, such as a door.

● Place your feet shoulder-width apart, heels about 16 inches from the wall. (Distance from the wall varies according to your height or length of legs.)

● Place the palms of your hands against the wall behind your buttocks to balance yourself while you bend your knees as if you're beginning to sit down in an invisible chair.

● With your feet still stationary on the floor, brace your back against the wall and keep inching down with bent knees until your thighs are *parallel* and your lower legs are perpendicular to the floor; then remove your hand.

● Without support of your hands or anything else, try to maintain this position for 90 seconds. In the proper position, the tops of the thighs and the shins are forming 90-degree angles. Your lap is so flat, you could put a platter of seaweed Jell-O across your thighs and it wouldn't slip off. If your buttocks are too high on the wall, your legs won't have to work enough; if they're too low, you could strain your knees.

● It doesn't matter what you do with your arms as long as you don't use them to support your weight. You can rest them loosely at your sides, hold them out to the side, or raise them up over your head; or all of the above at various times during the 90 seconds to amuse yourself. To pass the time, you can try counting how many breaths you use in 90 seconds; you can listen to music; or you can talk; anything at all—as long as you remain stationary in this position for 90 seconds. Don't forget to breathe throughout!

● After 90 seconds have passed, put your hand behind you for support and rise up (or slide down the wall to the floor).

● Rest for 30 seconds. Walk slowly about the room, shaking your legs loosely; or sit down whimpering; sing a half-minute aria; or curse your coach—it doesn't matter what you do to rest, just be sure that within 30 seconds of the moment you stopped, you are back in position ready to begin part two of 90/90's.

● A few seconds before the 30-second mark, bring your feet 4 to 6 inches closer to the wall than where you started the first 90 seconds. Spread your feet wide apart so that each foot is pointing out at a 45-degree angle, with heels about 3 feet apart and toes about 4 feet apart. (Spread your legs as far apart as you can for this second position. The farther apart they are, the more you'll work the adductor muscles, thereby firming the flesh along the inside of the thigh.) The thighs must be parallel to the floor and the tops of the thighs and the shins still form 90-degree angles.

● Repeat steps 3 through 7 above; and you're finished with your 90/90's for the day.

CHAPTER 6

The Warm-up Month and The Basic Training Calendar

If this month appears ridiculously easy for you, move right on to Basic Training. Or if you are somewhere in between this first week of warm-up and Basic Training to begin with, start with the third week of warm-up. Otherwise, have patience. You are not training for a competition. You have no need to rush into Basic Training before you are ready. You are going to indulge in very minimal exercise in order to gradually introduce or reintroduce your muscles to activity.

A month from now, when you begin your Basic Training routine, you will be performing the full set of stretching exercises described and photographed on pages 67–77. And you will be doing the full set of exercises with weights as described and shown in the photographs on pages 91–125 of the Weight Training Manual. And you will be doing full 90/90's described on pages 78–79. And, of course, you will be putting in 15 minutes of nonstop aerobic activity a day. So you have to get ready. It is far better to go through this warm-up month with laughable ease than to throw yourself right into Basic Training and be forced to backtrack to warm-up because you find it's too tough.

The first two weeks of warm-up are intended to give your heart a chance to work lightly and to open up your cardiovascular vessels. And they will accustom you to the idea of devoting a certain amount of time each day to your body. Brainwash your body into the habit of daily attention. The second two weeks of warm-up will require about the same time as Basic Training itself though you will

not yet be doing your 15 minutes of aerobic exercise nonstop, you will not yet be working with weights, you will not yet be doing the full set of stretching exercises and you will not yet be doing a full 90/90.

To make this first month a little more interesting, feel free to substitute bicycling or swimming or skipping rope whenever walking or running is indicated. Should you choose to swim, for instance, swim at a slow to moderate pace whenever walking is indicated, at a faster pace when running is called for. The same goes for cycling and skipping rope. Remember that running on treadmills and the use of stationary bicycles are not only permissible, but recommended.

Just as the exercises and the ratio of exercises in Basic Training are not arbitrary, this warm-up month has been carefully designed to prepare you for a full 90/90, a full weight workout and a full 15 minutes of aerobics. As soon as you think 90/90 work falls on Tuesdays, Thursdays and Saturdays in the warm-up, you are asked to do 90/90 work three days in a row. As soon as you think you know the order of the routine by heart, a new exercise will have slipped in. Follow each day's instructions carefully. You will be asked to refer to exercises in the stretching section (pp. 67–77) and in the Weight Training Manual (pp. 91–125). You will also be asked to perform aerobic work and additional exercises throughout the warm-up month.

Remember: Walk fast means just short of breaking into a run; run means run at any speed.

Warm-up: First Week

MONDAY

1. Stretch 1a, p. 69. Hold 30 sec.
2. Stretch 5b, c, p. 73. Hold each 30 sec.
3. Stretch 4a, b, p. 72. Hold each 30 sec.
4. Walk 5 continuous min. as fast as possible—just short of breaking into a run. Measure the time precisely with a second hand.
5. As soon as you finish your near-run walk (within 30 sec.), lean against a wall for 15 sec. in the first 90/90 position (p. 78).

TUESDAY

1. Stretch 1c, d, p. 69. Hold each 30 sec.
2. Stretch 5a, p. 73. Hold 30 sec.
3. Stretch 7, p. 75. Hold 30 sec.
4. Stretch 8a, b, c, d, p. 76. 10 times each.
5. Stretch 9b, p. 77. 10 times.
6. Walk 5 continuous min. as fast as possible—just short of breaking into a run. Measure the time precisely with a second hand.

WEDNESDAY

1. Stretch 1a, b; 4a, b; 5b, c; 7, pp. 69–77. Hold each 30 sec.
2. Stretch 8e, f; 9a, b, pp. 76–77. 10 times each.
3. Walk 5 continuous min. as fast as possible—just short of breaking into a run. Measure the time precisely with a second hand.
4. As soon as you finish your near-run walk (within 30 sec.), lean against a wall for 15 sec. in the first 90/90 position; then stand up for 15 sec.; then lean against the wall for 15 sec. in the second 90/90 position (p. 78).

THURSDAY

1. Stretch 1c, d; 6a, b, c, d; 7, pp. 69–75. Hold each 30 sec.
2. Stretch 9a, b, p. 77. 10 times each.
3. Do 10 bent-legged sit-ups. Follow instructions for exercise 15d, p. 125.
4. Do 5 half push-ups, knees on floor. Follow instructions for push-ups, p. 92.
5. Walk 5 continuous min. as fast as possible—just short of breaking into a run. Measure the time precisely with a second hand.

FRIDAY

1. Stretch 1a, b; 2; 4a, b; 7, pp. 69–75. Hold each 30 sec.
2. Stretch 8a, b, c, d, p. 76. 10 times each.
3. Do 10 bent-legged sit-ups. Follow instructions for exercise 15d, p. 125.
4. Do 5 half push-ups, knees on floor. Follow instructions for push-ups, p. 92.
5. Walk 5 continuous min. as fast as possible—just short of breaking into a run. Measure the time precisely with a second hand.
6. As soon as you finish your near-run walk (within 30 sec.), lean against a wall for 15 sec. in the first 90/90 position; then stand up for 15 sec.; then lean against the wall for 15 sec. in the second 90/90 position (p. 78).

SATURDAY

1. Stretch 1c, d; 2; 4a, b; 5a; 6a, b, c, d; 7, pp. 69–75. Hold each 30 sec.
2. Stretch 9a, b, p. 77. 10 times each.
3. Do 12 bent-legged sit-ups. Follow instructions for exercise 15d, p. 125.
4. Do 6 half push-ups, knees on floor. Follow instructions for push-ups, p. 92.
5. Walk 5 continuous min. as fast as possible—just short of breaking into a run. As soon as you finish, without stopping, run 30 sec. It doesn't matter how fast you run as long as you run continuously for 30 sec. Measure the time precisely with a second hand.

SUNDAY

Rest day

Warm-up: Second Week

Again, swimming, cycling or skipping rope may be substituted for running.

MONDAY

1. Stretch 1a, b; 2; 4a, b; 6a, b, c, d; 7, pp. 69–75. Hold each 30 sec.
2. Stretch 8e, f, p. 76. 10 times each.
3. Walk 1 min. fast.
   Run 30 sec.
   Walk 2 min. fast.
   Run 30 sec.
   Walk 1 min. slowly.
   This 5 min. should be continuous; measure the time precisely with a second hand.

TUESDAY

1. Stretch 1c, d; 2; 3; 5b, c; 7, pp. 69–75. Hold each 30 sec.
2. Stretch 9a, b, p. 77. 10 times each.
3. Do 15 bent-legged sit-ups. Follow instructions for exercise 15d, p. 125.
4. Do 10 half push-ups, knees on floor. Follow instructions for push-ups, p. 92.
5. Walk 1 min. slowly.
   Run 1 min.
   Walk 1 min. fast.
   This 3 min. should be continuous; measure the time precisely with a second hand.
6. Any time during the day you choose, lean against a wall for 30 sec. in the first 90/90 position (p. 78).

WEDNESDAY

1. Stretch 1b; 2; 3; 6a, b, c, d; 7, pp. 69–75. Hold each 30 sec.
2. Stretch 8a, b, c, d, p. 76. 10 times each.
3. Make a fist as hard as you can with both hands for 15 sec.; relax for 15 sec.; repeat for 15 sec.
4. Do 20 calf raises. Follow instructions for exercise 14b, p. 122.
5. Walk 1 min. slowly.
   Run 2 min.
   Walk 1 min. slowly.
   This 4 min. should be continuous. Measure the time precisely with a second hand.

THURSDAY

1. Stretch 1a, b; 4a, b; 5a; 7, pp. 69–75. Hold each 30 sec.
2. Stretch 8e, f, p. 76. 10 times each.
3. Do 12 half push-ups, knees on floor. Follow instructions for push-ups, p. 92.
4. Do 15 bent-legged sit-ups. Follow instructions for exercise 15d, p. 125.
5. Do side bends, 15 to each side. Follow instructions for exercise 15c, p. 125.
6. Walk 1 min. slowly.
   Run 2 min.
   Walk 1 min. fast.
   Run 2 min.
   Walk 1 min. slowly.
   This 7 min. should be continuous. Measure the time precisely with a second hand.

7. Any time during the day you choose, lean against a wall for 30 sec. in the first 90/90 position (p. 78).

FRIDAY

1. Stretch 1a, b, c, d; 5a, b, c; 7, pp. 69–75. Hold each 30 sec.
2. Stretch 9a, b, p. 77. 10 times each.
3. Make a fist as hard as you can with both hands for 15 sec.; relax for 15 sec.; repeat for 15 sec.
4. Do 20 calf raises. Follow instructions for exercise 14b, p. 122.
5. Walk 1 min. slowly.
   Run 2 min.
   Walk 1 min. slowly.
   Run 2 min.
   Walk 1 min. slowly.
   Run 2 min.
   Walk 1 min. slowly.
   This 10 min. should be continuous. Measure the time precisely with a second hand.
6. Any time during the day you choose, lean against a wall for 30 sec. in the first 90/90 position. Rest 30 sec., then lean against the wall in the second 90/90 position for 15 sec. (p. 78).

SATURDAY

1. Stretch 1c, d; 2; 3; 4a, b; 5a; 7, pp. 69–75. Hold each 30 sec.
2. Stretch 9a, b, p. 77. 10 times each.

3. Do 12 half push-ups, knees on floor. Follow instructions for push-ups, p. 92.
4. Do 18 bent-legged sit-ups. Follow instructions for exercise 15d, p. 125.
5. Do side bends, 15 to each side. Follow instructions for exercise 15c, p. 125.
6. Walk 30 sec. slowly.

Run 2 min.
Walk 30 sec. slowly.
Run 2 min.
Walk 30 sec. slowly.
Run 2 min.
Walk 2 min. slowly.
This 9½ min. should be continuous. Measure the time precisely with a second hand.
7. Any time during the day you

choose, lean against a wall for 30 sec. in the first 90/90 position. Rest 30 sec., then lean against the wall in the second 90/90 position for 15 sec. (p. 78).

SUNDAY

Rest day

Warm-up: Third Week

Again, swimming, cycling or skipping rope may be substituted for running.

MONDAY

1. Stretch 1a, b, c, d; 3; 6a, b, c, d; 7, pp. 69–75. Hold each 30 sec.
2. Stretch 8a, b, c, d, p. 76. 10 times each.
3. Make a fist as hard as you can with both hands for 15 sec.; relax for 15 sec.; repeat for 15 sec.
4. Do side bends, 20 to each side. Follow instructions for exercise 15c, p. 125.
5. Do 20 calf raises. Follow instructions for exercise 15c, p. 125.
6. Walk 2 min. slowly; run 2 min. Walk 2 min. fast; run 2 min. Walk 2 min. fast; run 2 min. Walk 2 min. fast; run 2 min. Walk 2 min. fast; run 2 min. This 20 min. should be continuous. Measure the time precisely with a second hand.
7. Any time during the day you choose, lean against a wall

for 45 sec. in the first 90/90 position (p. 78).

TUESDAY

1. Stretch 1c, d; 2; 5a; 7, pp. 69–75. Hold each 30 sec.
2. Stretch 9a, b, p. 77. 10 times each.
3. Do 20 bent-legged sit-ups. Follow instructions for exercise 15d, p. 125.
4. Do leg raises for 20 continuous sec. Follow instructions for exercise 15a, p. 124.
5. Do 15 half push-ups, knees on floor. Follow instructions for push-ups, p. 92.
6. Run 2 min.; walk 1 min. slowly.
Run 2 min.; walk 1 min. slowly.
Run 2 min.; walk 1 min. slowly.
Run 2 min.; walk 1 min. slowly.
Run 2 min.; walk 1 min. slowly.
This 15 min. should be continuous. Measure the time precisely with a second hand.
7. Any time during the day you

choose, lean against a wall for 20 sec. in the first 90/90 position. Rest 20 sec., then lean against the wall for another 20 sec. Rest 20 sec., then lean against the wall for a third 20 sec. in the first 90/90 position (p. 78).

WEDNESDAY

1. Stretch 1a, b; 3; 4a, b; 6a, b, c, d; 7, pp. 69–75. Hold each 30 sec.
2. Stretch 8e, f, p. 76. 10 times each.
3. Make a fist as hard as you can with both hands for 15 sec.; relax for 15 sec.; repeat for 15 sec.; relax for 15 sec.; repeat for 15 sec.; relax for 15 sec.; repeat for 15 sec.
4. Do side bends, 25 to each side. Follow instructions for exercise 15c, p. 125.
5. Do 25 calf raises. Follow instructions for exercise 14b, p. 122.
6. Run 3 min.; walk 1 min. slowly.
Run 3 min.; walk 1 min. slowly.

Run 3 min.; walk 1 min. slowly.

Run 3 min.; walk 1 min. slowly.

This 15 min. should be continuous. Measure the time precisely with a second hand.

7. Any time during the day you choose, lean against a wall for 50 sec. in the first 90/90 position (p. 78).

THURSDAY

1. Stretch 1a, b, c, d; 3; 5a; 7, pp. 69–75. Hold each 30 sec.
2. Stretch 9a, b, p. 77. 10 times each.
3. Do 25 bent-legged sit-ups. Follow instructions for exercise 15d, p. 125.
4. Do leg raises for 20 continuous sec. Follow instructions for exercise 15a, p. 124.
5. Do side bends, 25 to each side. Follow instructions for exercise 15c, p. 125.
6. Do 16 half push-ups, knees on floor. Follow instructions for push-ups, p. 92.
7. Run 6 min.; walk 2 min. slowly.
   Run 4 min.; walk 1 min. slowly.
   Run 2 min.; walk 1 min. slowly.
   Run 1 min.; walk 1 min.

slowly.

Run 1 min.; walk 1 min. slowly.

This 20 min. should be continuous. Measure the time precisely with a second hand.

8. Any time during the day you choose, lean against a wall for 30 sec. in the first 90/90 position. Rest 15 sec., then lean against the wall for 30 sec. in the second 90/90 position (p. 78).

FRIDAY

1. Stretch 1c, d; 2; 3; 4a, b; 6a, b, c, d; 7, pp. 69–75. Hold each 30 sec.
2. Stretch 8a, b, c, d, p. 76. 10 times each.
3. Make a fist as hard as you can with both hands for 20 sec.; relax for 10 sec.; repeat for 20 sec.; relax for 10 sec.; repeat for 20 sec.
4. Do 25 calf raises. Follow instructions for exercise 14b, p. 122.
5. Run 7½ min.; walk 2 min. slowly.
   Run 7½ min.
   This 17 min. should be continuous. Measure the time precisely with a second hand.
6. Any time during the day you choose, lean against a wall

for 55 sec. in the first 90/90 position (p. 78).

SATURDAY

1. Stretch 1a, b; 3; 5a, b, c; 6a, b, c, d, pp. 69–75. Hold each 30 sec.
2. Stretch 9a, b, p. 77. 10 times each.
3. Do 30 bent-legged sit-ups. Follow instructions for exercise 15d, p. 125.
4. Do leg raises for 30 continuous sec. Follow instructions for exercise 15a, p. 124.
5. Do side bends, 30 to each side. Follow instructions for exercise 15c, p. 125.
6. Do 18 half push-ups, knees on floor. Follow instructions for push-ups, p. 92.
7. Run 10 min.; walk 2 min. slowly.
   Run 5 min.
   This 17 min. should be continuous. Measure the time precisely with a second hand.
8. Any time during the day you choose, lean against a wall for 1 min. in the first 90/90 position. Rest 30 sec., then lean against the wall for 30 sec. in the second 90/90 position (p. 78).

SUNDAY

Rest day

Warm-up: Fourth Week

Repeat the third week, day for day. Now the first day of this fourth week will seem easy to you after completing the more difficult days at the end of the third week, and especially after Sunday's rest.

If you have now successfully completed the last 2 weeks of warm-up, you are ready to move on to Basic Training. If you were not able to complete these 2 weeks, DO NOT move on. Persist

until you can complete the third and fourth weeks as outlined (i.e., 2 weeks of the third-week program), then continue on to the Basic Training program that follows.

The Basic Training Calendar

The Basic Training program consists of four kinds of activity, as shown here. They are *stretching exercises*, for which proper technique is essential and is explained on pp. 67–77; *aerobic workouts*, which may include any or all of the following: running, swimming, cycling, skipping rope, rowing, cross-country skiing (see pp. 38–43 for technique and advice); workouts with *weights*, for which you can find illustrations in the Weight Training Manual (see pp. 91–125); and *90/90's*, described on pp. 78–79.

Six of your days are devoted to aerobics and 90/90's and stretching; two days are for weight training. One day a week, preferably the same day each week, is for rest. This is your day off from Basic Training.

Day 1

Stretch 5 min. (perform all required exercises on pp. 67–77).
Warm-up 2 min. Slowly start your aerobic activity and gradually increase your pace until you are ready to work at your magic pulse rate number.
Aerobics 15 min. nonstop at required pulse (80% of 220 minus your age).
Stretch 5 min. (perform all required exercises on pp. 67–77).
90/90 3 min. (pp. 78–79).
TOTAL TIME: 30 min.

Day 2

Stretch 5 min. (perform all required exercises on pp. 67–77).
Warm-up 2 min. Slowly start your aerobic activity and gradually increase your pace.
Aerobics 15 min. nonstop at required pulse rate.
Stretch 5 min. (all required exercises).
Weight Training (perform all required exercises on pp. 91–125 (approximate time: 30 min.).
90/90 3 min. (pp. 78–79).
TOTAL TIME: 60 min.

Day 3

Stretch 5 min. (all required exercises).
Warm-up 2 min. Slowly start your aerobic activity and gradually increase your pace.
Aerobics 15 min. nonstop at required pulse rate.
Stretch 5 min. (all required exercises).
90/90 3 min. (pp. 78–79).
TOTAL TIME: 30 min.

Day 4

Stretch 5 min. (all required exercises).
Warm-up 2 min. Slowly start your aerobic activity and gradually increase your pace.
Aerobics 15 min. nonstop at required pulse rate.
Stretch 5 min. (all required exercises).
90/90 3 min. (pp. 78–79).
TOTAL TIME: 30 min.

Day 5

Stretch 5 min. (all required exercises).
Warm-up 2 min. Slowly start your aerobic activity and gradually increase your pace.
Aerobics 15 min. nonstop at required pulse rate.
Stretch 5 min. (all required exercises).
Weight Training (perform all required exercises on pp. 91–125, approximately 30 min).
90/90 3 min. (pp. 78–79).
TOTAL TIME: 60 min.

Day 6

Stretch 5 min. (all required exercises).
Warm-up 2 min. Slowly start your aerobic activity and gradually increase your pace.
Aerobics 15 min. nonstop at required pulse rate.
Stretch 5 min. (all required exercises).
90/90 3 min. (pp. 78–79).
TOTAL TIME: 30 min.

Day 7

Rest Day
TOTAL TIME PER WEEK: 240 min., or 4 hrs.; or an average of 30 min. a day (except weight training days), with one full day of rest.

PART III
THE MANUALS

CHAPTER 7

The Weight-Training Manual

These are the strengthening exercises required of all Basic Training athletes twice a week. I will take you step by step through each exercise at each required station for each muscle group. And I will describe to you with words and with photographs precisely how to position your body and how to proceed with proper form at each station. Don't be afraid to ask someone at your weight room if you are confused about form or amount of weight or anything at all. On the other hand, keep in mind that some people who work in weight rooms don't know what they're talking about; and nine out of ten of those who do know the technical information will translate it in diluted form to a woman! Remember that merely going through the motions, as I see so many people doing in fitness clubs, won't do a thing for you. The average trainer in such a club not only will not encourage you to push to the point of intensity, but might also advise you to slack off if he sees you working hard on the pretext that "women shouldn't" or "women don't need to" or other such folderol. So until your workouts are second nature to you, take this manual along with you to the weight room and imitate the form for each muscle group. Follow the instructions exactly. If two exercises are given under one muscle group, do both. You must perform every exercise outlined here for the 15 muscle groups—your only choice is which type of equipment you're going to use. Later on, if you are enjoying your weight workouts and

would like to extend them, you might want to add some of the variations described in the Advanced Weight-Training Manual to your resistance work. But right now, you can feel tremendous satisfaction in performing the basics twice a week. As a matter of fact, many professional athletes never attempt to go beyond these basic exercises. The key is to be thorough and hit all 15 muscle groups intensely twice a week. If you can do this, there will be no need to expand your weight training.

As we've learned, resistance work is lifting or pressing against weights or weighted resistance in order to contract a muscle group. The contraction should be intense enough so that you can perform only 12 contractions with the weight or resistance you are using. (You will be asked to perform more than 12 repetitions of exercises that strengthen a muscle group without using weights—such as sit-ups.) When the twelfth contraction is squeezed out, that muscle group is stimulated to grow. If you are worried about excessive muscular growth ("bulging biceps"), don't be. A minuscule percentage of the female population has the hormonal potential to develop considerable muscle mass. As discussed earlier, most women do not have enough testosterone (the muscle size-building hormone) to build muscles of any considerable bulk. Cosmetically, a woman's resistance work affords firmer, tauter, stronger muscles, not unsightly mass.

A resistance session may take half an hour.

Still, it is not continuous work—each exercise is so intense as to last less than one minute. Of course, there can and will be soreness after intense muscle workouts. (I find that high heat, such as a whirlpool bath or a very hot shower, immediately following my weight workout will spare me some soreness the next day.) If you don't feel *some* soreness or burning sensations after your weight workouts— every time—you're not working hard enough. Also, you will feel more soreness doing Nautilus work, as opposed to free weights or Universal machines. This is because the Nautilus machines are designed to resist your muscles while you lower the weight (negatives) as well as when you lift it. Nautilus stretches the muscles more. With the other two systems, gravity actually helps you lower the weight, even when you try to slowly control it on the way down.

Sharp, knifelike pain during a weight workout is not healthy soreness or burning, however. If you feel an unbearable pain in your shoulder, for instance, skip the shoulder exercises for a week or so, work the rest of the body, and test out your shoulder after it's had rest.

In addition to heat after weight work, you need to warm the muscles and "prime" them for the heavy work they are about to perform *before* weight work. Instead of applying heat, warm them from the inside by raising your pulse rate. Ride 4 or 5 minutes on a stationary bike, skip rope for a couple of minutes, do 100 quick jumping jacks or do 30 quick sit-ups—any fast-paced activity for 2 to 5 minutes so that you break a light sweat, your pulse goes over at least 100 beats per minute, and your muscles are warmed. Then go to the weights. This is strictly a warm-up and does not count in your 15 required minutes of aerobics.

Along with your 2 to 5 minutes of pulse-raising activity, do 12 push-ups before every weight-training session. This is to stretch out the chest and shoulder muscles, and give the arms, lower back and stomach a chance to stretch before hitting the hard stuff. Push-ups will give the entire upper body a chance to warm from the blood pumping through as you work. You may have always done knee push-ups and are convinced that you cannot do even one full push-up. That's OK. Try to imitate the

form precisely (see photograph) for a full push-up, anyway.

Start with the whole body on one plane, hands at shoulder width, elbows locked. Keeping elbows in close to the body, and eyes looking straight down at the floor, come down until your nose is within six inches of the floor. Do not touch any part of your body to the floor—and try not to arch your back. Push yourself back up until your elbows lock again. If you absolutely cannot perform one push-up, start with sets of 16, 18, 20 half push-ups as you did in the warm-up month. If you can do 30 half push-ups, you can certainly do one full push-up.

If you can do 1 full push-up before starting Basic Training, you will be able to do 5 in a couple of weeks and you'll manage all 12 in a month, even if you have to do them in sets of 3 or 4 at a time. Eventually, however, you should do 12 continuous, quick, full pushups twice a week before weight training.

Intensity of the workout depends on your own level of fitness. Your ability to move greater amounts of weight depends on skeletal size, body weight, technique and recent weight-training background. Your ability to move quickly from muscle group to muscle group depends on cardiovascular conditioning, age and general fitness level. It may take a sixty-five-year-old woman who is not capable of great strength only 15 minutes to go through the 15 basic muscle groups until muscular growth is stimulated everywhere. But a strong twenty-five-year-old may need 45 minutes to go through the same basic 15 groups in order to reach the necessary intensity for her.

As you become more experienced with weights, try to become more creative. I have started you out looking for the right essentials, but you will soon know when to add a thirteenth repetition, when to try a few chin-ups as a warm-up, when to throw in a set of push-ups or dips between stations. I have been lifting weights of one description or another since age twelve (twenty years) and I can honestly say that I've never done precisely the same workout twice. If weight lifting is brand new to you, start off with the methodical 12 reps. When you feel comfortable with what you are trying to achieve, remember the basics and go off on your own. Remember the original concept of Basic Training is to teach you all the fundamentals and good habits of training so that they will eventually become second nature to you. Once they have become second nature, you are ready to expand and become creative with your workouts. In the Advanced Training Manual, you will find specific instructions and photographs for more difficult variations of the same exercises you will be doing here. If you consult Advanced Training for your weight workouts, DO NOT eliminate these Basic Training exercises. Just add some of the Advanced Training variations to your regular routine. Even world-class athletes begin their weight workouts with the basic set first.

You need not lift dumbbells to perform your weight training. There are three basic methods available to you: free weights, Universal gyms and Nautilus machines. It doesn't matter which you choose—or you may have access to two or all three systems. You can even do part of your workout with one and other muscle groups with another. For instance, you might like to work your upper body with free weights for more bulk and your lower body with Nautilus for more stretch. Regardless, do every exercise listed under any of the systems for each muscle group. And if, for example, you've done all the Nautilus work for the deltoids (shoulders) and want to add one or two dumbbell exercises for your shoulders, feel free. You can't do too much; you can only do too little.

1. Free Weights

Free weights refer to barbells and dumbbells and are called "free" because they are not attached to anything.

- *Pros:* Coordination and more raw power are developed using free weights because you have to control the angle of movement yourself. Free weights may be kept in the home and don't take up much room—an entire set could easily be stored under your bed.
- *Cons:* Free weights can be risky—only your strength supports them in the air and you might drop them if you don't exercise caution and control or if you're trying a weight that is very heavy for you for a certain muscle group. Free weights force your muscles to move through an extremely short arc, which can lead to explosive strength but also shortened (tight) muscle fibers. If you use free weights, expect a thicker, bulkier look than you would develop with Nautilus.
- *Accessibility:* Free weights provide the most accessible and inexpensive form of weight training. Barbells and dumbbells are available at most schools, Y's and health clubs. An adequate set of free weights can be purchased for under $30.

2. Universal Machines

Universal is a brand name for a single machine that offers "stations" at which you can work the 12 basic muscle groups.

- *Pros:* The Universal is very safe because all the weights are attached to a central machine and cannot fall on you if you let them go. Up to eight people can comfortably work out on one machine at a time, following each other from station to station.
- *Cons:* You must have a minimum space of approximately 64 square feet to allow room for the machine itself and a little leg room at each station. Like free weights the Universal forces your muscles to move through an extremely short arc. This leads to short, tight muscle fibers.
- *Accessibility:* Many health clubs, Y's, schools and other public facilities are beginning to replace their free weights with Universal machines. The extra money spent on a Universal

machine probably equals the extra money spent to replace the bars, weights and accessories misplaced when free weights are used. And no money need be spent on a safety supervisor that is advisable with free weights.

3. Nautilus Machines

Nautilus is a brand name for weight-lifting machines that allow a muscle group to meet variable resistance through a full range of movement. (Nautilus makes one machine for each major muscle group; you lie on a bench or sit on a seat and move weights attached to a pulley and a rotary cam.) This cam allows the amount of weight to change throughout the movement, so that the weight becomes heavier as your position of leverage improves, thus working the muscle group intensely at each stage of the movement. Nautilus measures the amount of weight you move at each station in numbers of plates, rather than in numbers of pounds; pounds are used in free weights and the Universal. Nautilus is not the only manufacturer of these types of rotary cam machines, although it was the first and is still the most popular. Other common brand names are Digger (from Canada) and Iron Man.

- *Pros:* The rotary cam, providing varying resistance throughout the movement according to your position of leverage, allows the muscle to work at maximum capacity at all points of movement. Nautilus is designed to allow each muscle group to work through an extremely wide arc so that the muscle has a chance to prestretch before it contracts fully—the muscles do not become as tight as when working on the Universal or free weights. Nautilus is very safe because, as on the Universal, the weights are attached to the machine and cannot get away from you, although accidents occasionally happen whereby a muscle group is torn when too much weight is being used and it cannot be controlled. Most Nautilus centers are run as one-to-one or nearly one-to-one programs so that you usually get the knowledge and the coaching of a trained expert each time you work out. You can isolate each muscle group more specifically on Nautilus than on any other type of weight equipment; there are straps and seat selections to hold your body still while you work one muscle group at a time.

- *Cons:* Nautilus requires an enormous amount of space. Each machine takes up about the same space as a dentist chair. Because each machine will only work one muscle group, you need a minimum of 15 machines.

- *Accessibility:* Public facilities generally do not offer Nautilus equipment, which is expensive. Each machine costs from $2,000 to $4,000. Nautilus equipment has become increasingly available at many health clubs and private Nautilus centers. However, these facilities are still much more expensive than those that offer free weights or Universal equipment, since the clubs have to charge a higher yearly membership fee in order to compensate for the expense of the equipment and the space.

Note: If you absolutely cannot afford to join an establishment where weight equipment is available and you cannot afford to purchase free weights, fashion makeshift weights at home. Use heavy smooth-edged bookends or bottles filled with sand to perform the free weight exercises. It will be more difficult to achieve the desired intensity or form this way, but you will still have a minor resistance workout, which is better than nothing.

THE RESISTANCE EXERCISES

I have found that performing the exercises in the following order produces the best results in the long run. If this order is not possible for you because of set procedures at your weight room, it is not crucial. Intense work on the 15 major muscle groups is the minimum requirement for Basic Training. However, I have added several other resistance exercises in Advanced Training—such as negative chins, negative dips, isometrics, etc.—in case you reach the point where an added exercise or two each session appeals to you.

Remember, one repetition is the full movement

of the weight—up and down again, out and back again, for example—and you are aiming to do 12 repetitions so that the twelfth one will be difficult enough to thoroughly exhaust that muscle group. (For exercises where no fixed weight is used, such as push-ups or leg raises, 12 is no longer the magic number; I have indicated how many reps to do in each of these cases.) And don't forget that negative work (eccentric contractions where you only lower a very heavy weight) makes great gains in strength. The trouble is that you usually need another person who is stronger than you at that moment to push the heavy weight up so that you can perform the negative in letting it down. Even when doing positives (both up and down reps), though, make sure to work with a heavy enough weight for each muscle group so that you have a lot of trouble getting that twelfth rep.

It is never advisable to work with free weights alone and, especially if you are a beginner with weights, it is difficult to manipulate the weights with effective form without a spotter. You must work with a dangerous amount of weight in order to work the lower body and even some of the upper body (the bench press, for instance). If free weights is the only system available to you, or if you decide to choose free weights, make a sure a competent partner assists you.

There are a couple of exercises which require another person's help. Don't feel embarrassed to ask someone in the weight room who might have a free minute to help hold your ankles or do whatever you need. Don't think that people will judge your strength or your body. What will impress them is that you know which muscles you want to work, that you work them hard and that you have great technique. I sometimes ask men who can lift five times more weight than I can to give me a hand— they are always more than happy to give a minute to someone who is concentrating seriously and

knows what she is doing. Your individual potential is exciting—don't compare yourself with others, and don't compare yourself with men.

Regardless of which system you choose, do every exercise in a slow and controlled motion. Experiment to find the right amount of weight or number of plates for each exercise. Then keep a log book or sheet to check off the amount of weight and the number of reps each weight workout. This way you are precise about how much weight is correct for each exercise and you can see your improvement as you get stronger and increase the weight or the reps. At some point, 12 reps will be too easy for a certain muscle group with a certain weight. But more weight will be too tough. In this case, do 15 or 17 reps until even they become easy, then you will be ready to increase the weight. And there will be some days when you can't get 10 reps with the weight you usually handle for 12. Don't get down on yourself. Realize that you're not quite as strong that day and get back to 12 the next time—but get as many as you can. It's OK to underachieve now and then because of physical fatigue but you should put 100 percent of your willpower into your effort every time.

Imitate the photos and follow the written instructions precisely. Instructions to start with the elbows locked or slightly bent are not superficially thrown in; each minuscule change in position has an effect on the muscle being worked. It doesn't matter what you wear to lift weights. I usually wear shorts and a T-shirt. You must always wear shoes when doing any type of weight lifting. Lifting barefoot can be dangerous; one slip of a foot and you might lose control of the weight—or lose control of your body around the machines.

One last thing before you begin. Don't forget to breathe while you are lifting weights. Inhale during the "in" or "down" phase of the rep; exhale during the "out" or "up" phase for that little extra effort.

1. LOWER BACK

Free Weights   1a   Lie on the floor face down. Hold a light weight (5 to 10 pounds) with both hands on the sides of the weight, lightly touching the back of your neck. Start with your elbows out to the sides and your chin 2 inches off the floor. Keep your legs and hips flat on the floor and keep your head and back on the same plane throughout—don't bend your neck. Lift your upper body off the floor until your eyes look straight out across the room; hold that position for 1 second, then lower yourself until your chin is again 2 inches off the floor. Repeat 12 times. If this exercise strains your back to the point that it hurts for hours after your workout, do this exercise, as instructed, without the weight. Once you can handle 12 reps easily without the weight, go back to using a light weight.

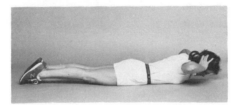 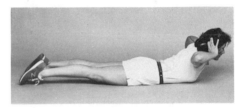

Free Weights   1b   Hang over the edge of a bench or bed, face down, with your hips just over the edge. Have someone press down firmly on your heels or calves so that your legs and hips can remain stationary. Clasp your hands behind your neck, elbows out, and start curled under the bench as far as you can go. Lift your upper body up until your eyes look straight out across the room. Hold there for 1 second, then lower yourself slowly until you are curled under the bench again. Repeat 12 times.

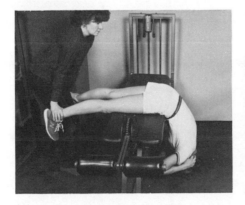 

Universal	**1c**	Some Universal set-ups offer a station where you can perform the second exercise (**1b**) under Free Weights above without the necessity of someone holding your legs down. Just hook your heel under the roller, plant your other foot against the plate and proceed precisely as described above under (**1b**). If your Universal does not offer this station, do both Free Weight exercises (**1a**) and (**1b**).

Nautilus	**1d**	Hip and Back Machine: Lie on your back, legs hooked over the rollers just above the knees, buttocks way down at the edge of the bench, hands gripping the side handles. Start with your feet flexed up; press down slowly with both legs, keeping your back flat, until your knees lock, your toes point, and the weights touch the top and can be pressed no farther. Keep the left leg down all the way, toes pointed, and bring the right leg back up (foot flexed) until the knee is as close to your chest as possible. Hold that position for 1 second, then press down until both legs are again locked at the bottom. Repeat with the left leg and alternate until you have done 12 reps with each leg.

 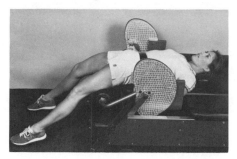 

Nautilus	**1e**	Many Nautilus centers provide a Roman Chair. Hang face down, hips just over the edge, calves or heels hooked under the rollers to brace you. Then proceed exactly as described in the second exercise (**1b**) under Free Weights above. If you have no Roman Chair, add the second Free Weight exercise after you finish the hip and back machine above.

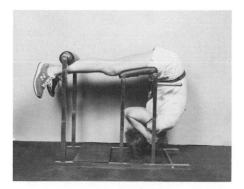 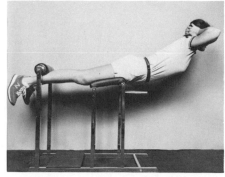

2. LATISSIMUS DORSI (the large fanlike muscle which laterally covers most of the back)

Free Weights   2a   Stand with your feet 3 feet apart, knees slightly bent. Bend forward at the waist with a dumbbell in your right hand until your back is parallel to the floor. Rest your left hand on your left thigh. Start with the dumbbell at the left shin; pull it across your body and up to your right armpit, keeping the elbow in close to the body. Keep your upper body stationary while your arm works. Lower it slowly to your left shin again. Work the right arm consecutively 12 times, then work the left arm. Look straight down at the floor throughout.

Free Weights   2b   Stand with feet 3 feet apart, knees slightly bent. Bend forward at the waist until your back is parallel to the floor, holding a dumbbell down by the sides of each calf. Keeping the upper body stationary and the elbows in close to the body, pull both dumbbells up slowly until they touch their respective armpit. Lower both slowly simultaneously.

Universal   2c   Kneel on the floor so that the bar is directly above you. Grab the bar palms down at each end of the bar, elbows locked. Bend your neck so that your head falls forward. Pull down slowly until the bar touches the back of your neck; hold the bar there for 1 second, then let it back up slowly until elbows lock again. Perform these lat pulldowns with a smooth, fluid motion throughout—do not jerk the bar or let it fly up.

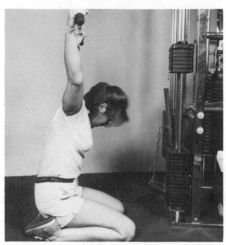 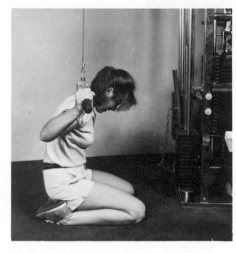

Universal   2d   Sit on the floor so that the bar is directly above you. Reach up and grab the bar palms up with your hands as close together as possible. The bar may be too high for you to reach sitting, so stand and pull it down to your sitting position to begin. Start with your elbows locked, feeling as though the bar is pulling you up off the floor. Keeping your elbows in close to the body, pull the bar down slowly until you touch your chest. Hold the bar there for 1 second, then let it back up slowly until the elbows lock again. (This exercise will also work the biceps extensively.)

 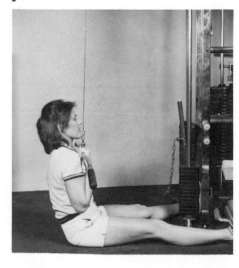

Nautilus **2e** Sit in the pullover machine with the seat at such a height that your shoulders meet the middle of the shoulder pads. Stretch back your arms and place your elbows on the elbow pads. Press forward with your elbows until your hands come around to waist level. Hold both hands there for 1 second, then let the right arm back slowly while holding the left arm all the way down. Once the right arm is back in the original stretched position, press it down slowly until it is at waist level again. Now hold it there while the left arm works. Alternate arms until you have done 12 reps with each. Keep your back and head firmly against the back pad throughout. Do not squirm with your upper body; move your arms only. Your machine may not allow you to work one arm at a time. If not, proceed with both arms simultaneously as instructed above.

Nautilus **2f** Sit in the upper torso machine, strapped in. Lean very far forward with your legs behind you to each side. Grab the bar palms down at each end and proceed exactly as described under the first Universal exercise (**2c**) above.

Nautilus

2g   Sit in the upper torso machine, strapped in. Both thighs should be touching and your back and head should be pressing firmly against the back pad. Grab the bar above you, palms up, with your hands as close together as possible. Proceed exactly as described under the second Universal exercise **(2d)** above.

3. DELTOIDS (shoulders)

Free Weights

3a   Lateral raises. Stand with your feet 2 feet apart, a light dumbbell in each hand lightly touching each other in front of you. Elbows should be slightly bent. Simultaneously raise both dumbbells until both arms are parallel to the floor. Slowly lower them back to the starting position, the elbows as close to locking as possible without actually doing so. Try to keep your body perfectly still throughout, only moving your arms.

Free Weights

3b Dumbbell press. Stand with feet 2 feet apart, a dumbbell in each hand at the outside of each shoulder. Keeping your elbow close in to the body, press up slowly with the right arm until the elbow locks. As you are lowering the right dumbbell to the starting position, press up slowly with the left. Do 12 reps on each arm. Keep the whole body stationary; do not use your back or lean back to use your chest—use only your arms.

Universal

3c Military press. Sit on the stool with the bars right above each shoulder—not in front of or in back of the shoulders. The height of the stool should allow the bar to be at your shoulder height—not too far above or below it. Keeping your elbows in close to the body, slowly push straight up until your elbows lock. Lower slowly until you are just 1 inch from touching the weights down and repeat. You need to support the weights on your own at the bottom of the rep rather than resting for an instant while they touch down.

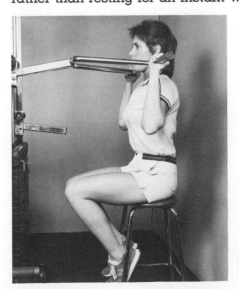 

Nautilus   **3d**   Sit in the deltoid machine, strapped in, the seat at such a height that your forearms are parallel with the floor when you begin. Hold each handle with the tops of your wrists pressed against the pads. Press up slowly until your elbows reach shoulder level. Hold there for 1 second, keeping your back and head pressed firmly against the back pad throughout. Then slowly lower the left arm to within 1 inch of touching the weights down and bring it back up to shoulder height. Hold the left arm up while the right arm goes up and down. Don't touch the weights back down until you have done 12 reps on each arm. Or you can work both arms simultaneously. Keep your wrists firm throughout instead of breaking your wrists and cheating by using your forearms.

Nautilus   **3e**   Sit in the deltoid machine, strapped in. Reach for the handles with both hands (the handles should be at your ear level—move the chair up or down accordingly). Keeping your elbows in close to your head and keeping your back and head pressed firmly on the back pad, proceed exactly as described under the Universal military press above **(3c).**

4. PECTORALS (chest)

Free Weights   **4a**   Bench press. Lie on your back on a bench so that you can easily reach up to grab the barbell from the rack or from a friend who will hand it to you. Grip the bar at shoulder width and start with the bar lightly touching your chest. Your feet should be up on the bench to avoid back injury and someone should be spotting you to catch the weight in case you lose control of it. Keep your elbows close in to your head, slowly pressing up until your elbows lock. Lower slowly until the bar lightly touches your chest again. If you have only dumbbells, no barbell, perform the same bench press holding one heavy dumbbell with two hands as pictured here. This narrow grip will also work the triceps extensively. Study the Universal bench press photo **(4c)** to see how this press looks with a bar instead of a dumbbell.

 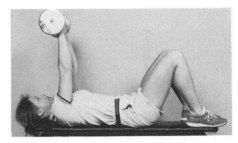

Free Weights   **4b**   Standing flies. Stand with a dumbbell in each hand, held straight out from your waist in front of you, dumbbells touching. Keeping both elbows pressed tightly into the sides of your waist, swing the dumbbells simultaneously as far out to each side as possible. Keep your forearms parallel with the floor throughout so that they form right angles with your upper arms. Bring the dumbbells back in so that they touch. Repeat for 12 reps.

Universal

4c There is a bench press station on the Universal. Proceed as described under the bench press exercise (**4a**) of Free Weights above *except* for two things: (1) A bar will not touch your chest. You will start with a handle at either side of your chest. (2) Do not touch the weights all the way down at the end of each rep; let the weights come down within one inch of touching down and press back up. With free weights, you can touch the weights back down to your chest because you are still supporting the bar, but if the Universal weights touch back down you do no work for that moment.

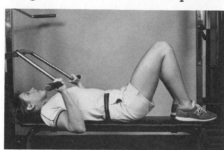 

Nautilus

4d Sit in the chest machine at such a height that your forearms form a 90-degree angle to your upper arms when performing the exercise. You may need a pad under you or in back of you if you can't quite reach. Keeping your back and head pressed firmly against the back pad, press your hands and elbows around toward each other in front of you. Your elbows should come as close to each other as possible in this position while the right arm goes slowly back to the original stretched starting position and slowly comes forward to join the left arm again. Then hold the right arm there while the left arm works. Continue until you have done 12 reps on each side. Or you can work both arms simultaneously for the 12 reps.

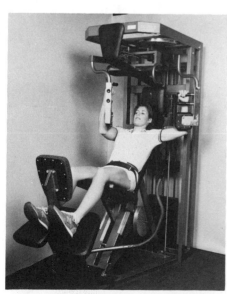 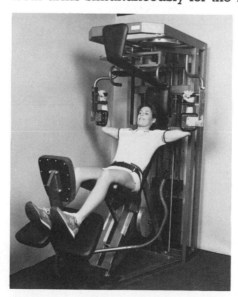 

Nautilus   **4e**   Sit in the chest machine, strapped in. Press forward with your feet against the pad in front of you. This will bring two handles up on either side of you. Keeping your elbows out from your body, push the handles out in front of you with the heels of your hands until your elbows lock. Now take your feet off the pad and let them dangle off the seat while you work. Elbows out, slowly bring the handles back toward your chest and as far past your chest as they will go. Then push both handles forward until your elbows are locked again. When you are finished put your feet back up on the pad to lower the weights all the way back down.

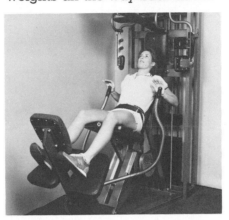 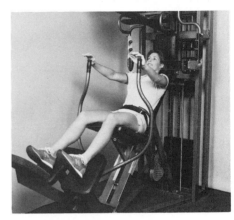

5. TRAPEZIUS (between the shoulder and neck)

Free Weights   **5a**   Stand with your feet 2 feet apart. Hold a dumbbell in each hand by each side. Keeping your elbows locked, shrug your shoulders simultaneously as high as they will go. Try to touch your ears with your shoulders. The shrug, both up and down, should be slow and smooth.

Universal

5b Use the bicep bar. Stand upright, holding the bar palms down in front of you at hip height. Your hands should be as close together as possible. Keep your body perfectly still and draw the bar up to your chin. Your elbows should be as high as possible throughout.

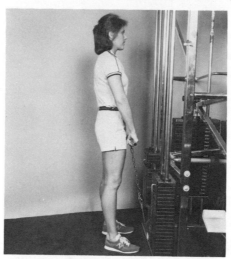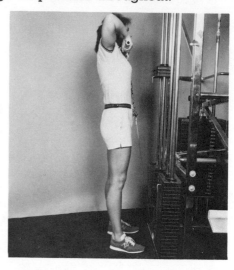

Nautilus

5c Nautilus does make a machine for shrugs but it is a rarity at most centers. The machine allows you to sit and place your forearms under pads and then work the trapezius muscles by shrugging the shoulders. If you do not have this machine, do the exercise described under Free Weights above (5a)—even shrugs without dumbbells can be effective if you do at least 30 reps.

6. TRICEPS (back of the upper arm)

Free Weights

6a Bend over at the waist until your back is parallel with the floor, knees bent. With a dumbbell in each hand, pull your elbows up behind you so that they touch either side of your waist. Your forearms should be 90 degrees to your upper arms so that the weights hang toward the floor. Keeping your upper arms and elbows absolutely still and your elbows pinned in close to your waist, push straight back with your forearms until your arms are straight behind you. Slowly bring your forearms back to the 90-degree position again. If you lose your balance doing both arms together, do one arm at a time, holding onto something solid with your free hand for balance.

Free Weights   **6b**   Stand up, feet 2 feet apart. Hold one dumbbell behind your neck with both hands; don't touch the weight to your neck. Point your elbows straight up in the air. Press up with both hands until the dumbbell is straight over your head and your elbows are locked. Lower the dumbbell slowly, keeping your upper arms and elbows absolutely still throughout, using only your forearms. You can do this one arm at a time with a lighter weight.

Universal

6c Stand at the lat pull-down bar. Grab the bar palms down with your hands as close together as possible—thumbs on top of the bar, not under. Start with the bar at your chest, your elbows pressed in close to your body. Press straight down until your elbows lock. Slowly let the bar come back up to chest level before the next rep. Keep your upper arms and elbows absolutely straight and close in to your body throughout.

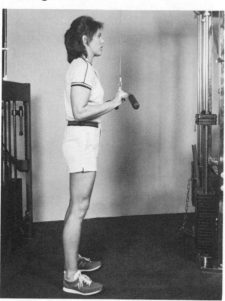
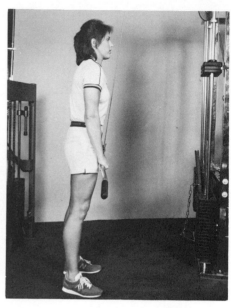

Nautilus

6d Sit in the dual tricep machine facing the pads with the seat at such a height that your forearms start at a 90-degree angle to your upper arms. Keeping your elbows on the pads, press down with both hands until your elbows lock. Keep the right elbow locked while the left arm bends all the way back to the starting position and then presses out to join the right again. Then keep the left elbow locked while you work the right arm. Continue until you have completed 12 reps on each arm. Keep your back and head pressed firmly on the back pad throughout. If your machine does not enable you to work one arm at a time, work both arms simultaneously as instructed for one arm.

7. BICEPS (front of upper arm)

Free Weights **7a** Stand with feet 2 feet apart, knees locked, a dumbbell in each hand. Hold the dumbbells down on your thighs, palms up, elbows locked. Dig your elbows in at your waist. Keep your back and upper arms absolutely still, and elbows tight in at your waist, while you pull the dumbbells up with your forearms until each touches its respective shoulder. Lower the dumbbells slowly until your elbows lock again. Looking in a mirror when doing this exercise will help you to maintain your form.

Free Weights **7b** Start in the exact same position as exercise **7a**. This time work one arm at a time. As one arm is lowering, the other arm should be curling up toward the shoulder.

Universal

7c Stand at the bicep curl bar, holding the bar palms up, hands shoulder width apart. Start with the bar touching your thighs, elbows locked. Curl the bar up to your chest with the exact same motion described under Free Weights above. Keep your back and upper arms absolutely still while your forearms work and keep your elbows tight in at the waist.

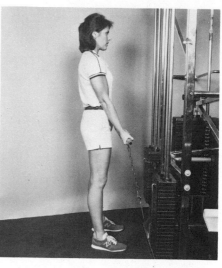

Nautilus

7d Sit facing the pads in the dual bicep machine; the seat level should be at such a height that your arms lie flat across the pads, elbows locked, to begin. Gripping the handles palms up, slowly curl the handles up until they touch under your chin. Hold the right handle under your chin while your left arm lowers and curls up again. Then hold the left handle under your chin while the right arm works. Continue until you have done 12 reps with each arm. Keep your back and head firmly pressed against the back pad throughout. Your machine may not allow you to work one arm at a time. If so, follow the same instructions and work both arms simultaneously.

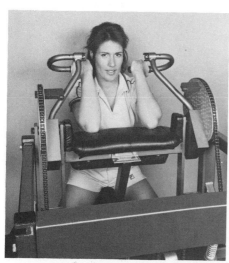 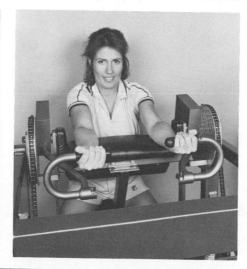 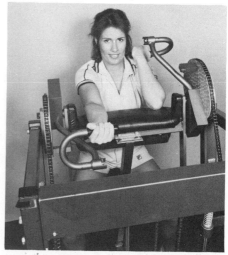

8. FOREARMS

Free Weights   **8a**   Hold a light dumbbell in your right hand, palm up. Rest your forearm on a bench with the wrist just over the edge or steady your right forearm by digging your right elbow into your waist and putting your left hand under your right forearm. Keeping your whole arm—except your wrist—stationary, let the wrist flop down as far as possible and then curl it back up as far as possible. After doing 12 reps with the right wrist, switch and do the left wrist.

Free Weights   **8b**   Do this same exercise with the palms down. You will have to use a lighter weight with the palms down.

Universal **8c** Stand facing the bicep bar. Hands shoulder-width apart, palms up, pull up the bar so that your forearms are parallel to the floor. Dig your elbows in at your waist and do not move them or your forearms throughout the exercise. Let your wrists break down so that the bar is as close to the floor as possible; then curl your wrist up so that the bar is as high as possible.

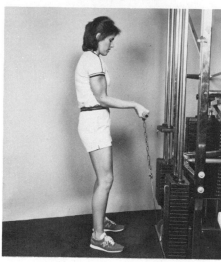 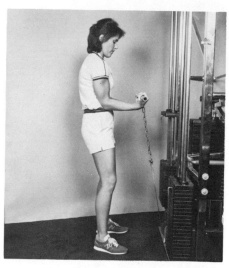

Universal **8d** When you finish 12 reps palms up, do 12 reps palms down (you will probably have to decrease the weight).

Universal **8e** Sometimes Universal offers a rolling bar where you stand gripping the bar with both hands and roll it forward or backward, palms down and palms up. Remember to keep your entire arm stationary, except the wrist.

Nautilus **8f** Sit in the dual bicep machine, prepared to perform bicep curls (p. 112, exercise **7d**). Use a very light weight and, instead of curling the handles all the way up to your shoulders, keep the entire arm stationary while you flex only the wrist. Rest your right elbow on the pad, wrist extended toward the handle, about 6 inches higher than your elbow. This way your wrist, palm up, will have to break down as far as possible using only wrist—no forearm. When you have done 12 reps with the right hand, work the left; then repeat the entire exercise palms down. There is an excellent forearm machine made by another company, Digger, which is often found at clubs that offer Nautilus. Use of this machine is described under Advanced Training, but you may certainly use it here in Basic Training if you have access to it. If you use the bicep machine, take a look at the photos of the Digger exercise under "forearms" in Advanced Training for form.

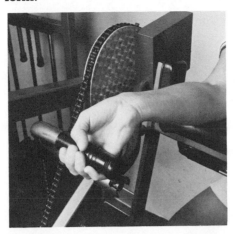

9. QUADRICEPS (front of thigh)

Free Weights

9a Stand, toes pointed out and heels 3 feet apart, with a barbell across the back of your shoulders (preferably) or with a dumbbell held on each shoulder. Slowly squat down, keeping your back and head in one position, until your thighs are parallel with the floor. (Going any lower than this may cause damage to the knees.) Then slowly press up to the standing position again, keeping your back and head in one position. And don't forget that your 90/90's also work the quadriceps.

Universal	**9b**	Sit with your feet on the lower pedals (some machines have only one set of pedals). Begin with your shins at a 90-degree angle to your thighs. You may have to adjust the seat to get this 90-degree angle, which is ideal for the quadriceps. (Compare this to the Universal angle for the buttocks [**11b**]). Keep your back pressed firmly against the seat back and then press out until your knees are just short of locking. Press out and come back in smoothly and slowly—do not jerk the weights for added momentum.

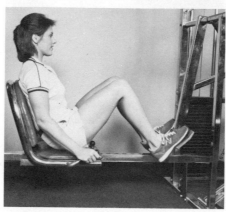 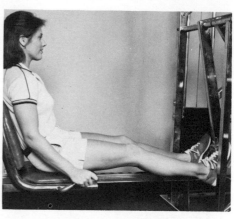

Universal	**9c**	Some weight rooms provide a separate Universal hamstring machine that has a leg extension station for quadriceps on it. If you are privy to this machine, proceed exactly as described below under the first Nautilus exercise (**9d**), which is a leg extension.

Nautilus	**9d**	Sit in the leg extension machine with your head back on the pad, hands gripping the side handles, the front of both ankles resting behind the rollers. Keep your entire back pressed flat against the seat-back throughout. Start with the weights pressed up 2 inches from the resting position; squeeze up slowly until your knees lock. Keep your feet flexed instead of pointing your toes in order to work the shin muscles too. Come back down slowly to within two inches of touching the weights back down. Press up again. You can work one quad at a time by hanging the nonworking leg out to the side of the seat. If you feel one quad is weaker or if you have any knee problem, working one leg at a time can help.

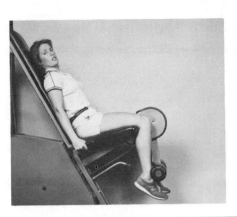
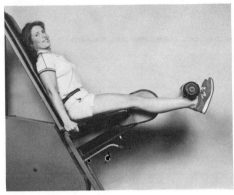

Nautilus	**9e**	There is a Nautilus leg press machine but it is not found at all centers. If you have access to one, proceed as described above under the first Univeral exercise **(9b).**

10. BICEPS FEMORIS (hamstrings—back of the thigh)

Free Weights	**10a**	Lie face down on the floor or on a bench. Bend your knees so that your feet are 6 inches off the floor. Have a friend slip a towel behind your heels and pull. As your friend applies steady, firm resistance, you pull with your heels against the towel until your heels touch your buttocks (or as closely as possible). As you lower your heels slowly, your friend should continue to apply resistance with the towel. Keep your hips flat on the ground throughout—the higher your buttocks go in the air, the less your hamstrings work. Lower your feet to within 6 inches of the floor before starting the next rep—do not touch the floor.

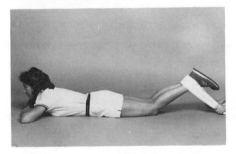

Universal	**10b**	Some weight rooms offer a Universal leg curl machine for the hamstrings. It looks and operates exactly like the Nautilus leg curl machine described below **(10c)**. If you do not have this machine, do the Free Weight exercise above **(10a)**.
Nautilus	**10c**	Lie face down on the hamstring machine, hands gripping the handles, knees just over the edge of the bench, heels under the two rollers. Start with the rollers pressed up so that the weights are 2 inches from touching down. Keeping your hips flat on the bench (do not let your buttocks rise up in the air), slowly squeeze up with your heels against the rollers until the rollers touch the buttocks (or come as close as possible). Lower the rollers slowly until you are just 2 inches from touching down. Lift your head up so that you are looking straight across the room throughout; this will help keep your hips down.

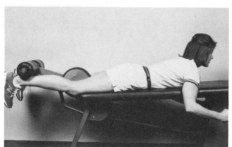 

11. GLUTEUS MAXIMUS (buttocks)

Free Weights	**11a**	Donkey kicks. Kneeling, place palms on the floor at shoulder width, elbows locked. Tuck your head under your body and reach your left knee up to touch your nose. Then kick one leg up behind you as high as you can—knee slightly bent—as you lift your eyes toward the ceiling. Each kick should be done intensely, almost violently, instead of slowly and smoothly like most of the weight exercises. Work the left leg for 30 consecutive kicks, then work the right leg. Light ankle weights (2½ to 5 pounds) will make this exercise even more effective. Clubs usually do not provide ankle weights; you will have to purchase your own. They attach around the ankle by a Velcro strip.

Universal	**11b**	Sit at the leg press station with your feet on the upper pedals (some machines have only one set of pedals). Start with your knees close to your chin, your thighs against your chest, the weights pressed out 2 inches from touchdown. To begin, press out slowly until your knees are almost locked. Come back in slowly, all the way, so that your knees are again close to your chin. In order to get the proper angle to work the buttocks, you may have to adjust the seat by sliding it closer to the weights. (Compare this to the Universal angle for the quadriceps [9b]).

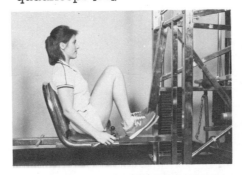
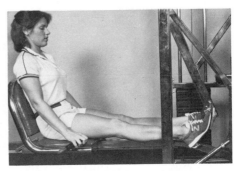

Nautilus	**11c**	If your Nautilus center has a leg press machine, move the seat forward from where you usually do quadricep leg presses so that your knees are close to your chin as you start. Then proceed as outlined in the Universal exercise above (11b). If you do not have this machine, do the next Nautilus exercise (11d). Or do the Free Weights exercise (11a).

Nautilus **11d** Although not designed for the buttocks, I find the leg extension machine can come in handy for this muscle group. Face the back seat of the machine, standing on your right leg. Lean over the seat on your stomach and hook your left leg under the outside roller. The roller should catch your calf. Push the roller up in back of you as high as you can, then lower it but don't touch the weights all the way back down before starting the next rep. After 12 repetitions, go to the other side and work your right leg.

12. ADDUCTORS (inside of thigh)

Free Weights **12a** Lie on the floor on your back. Prop yourself up on your elbows, hands under your buttocks. Knees locked, lift your legs 6 inches off the floor, legs touching. Slowly, always six inches off the floor, spread your legs as far as they will possibly go. Push for an extra inch and hold there. This last stretch is most important in working this muscle group. Without touching the floor, repeat 15 times. If you can maintain form, do as many as you can. (If possible, buy a pair of ankle weights—small weighted belts that wrap around your ankles and are secured with Velcro—to use for this and other exercises.)

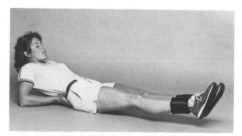 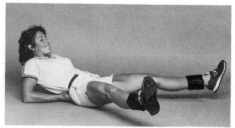

Universal Do the above exercise (12a).

Nautilus Do the above exercise (12a).

13. ABDUCTORS (outside of the thigh)

Free Weights **13a** Kneel on the floor, palms down at shoulder width. Lift your left leg, knee completely bent, to the side until your knee is as high as your back—imagine a dog lifting its leg at a hydrant. Keep your thigh and knee stationary while you kick your lower leg straight out to the side. Kick 30 times consecutively with the left leg, then work the right leg. Two things can make this exercise even more effective: (1) look in a mirror to make sure your knee is high and stationary throughout; (2) strap an ankle weight onto the kicking leg.

Free Weights **13b** Lie on your right side on the floor. Lean on one elbow, propping your head up with that hand. Put the other hand on the floor in front of you, palm down. Start with the left leg 3 inches in the air, up from the right leg. Lift your left leg up, knee locked, as high as possible—straight up toward the ceiling would be ideal. Lower your leg to 3 inches from your right leg—don't touch legs. Repeat 30 kicks consecutively with your left leg, then work the right leg. This exercise should be done slowly, whereas the first exercise (**13a**) should be done with quick kicks. An ankle weight on the kicking leg would make this exercise more effective also.

Universal and Nautilus Neither Universal nor Nautilus makes equipment specifically to work the abductors (although Nautilus will soon have one on the market). These muscles at the outside of the thigh are a constant complaint by women, for good reason—they get no work in everyday activity. Do both of the exercises under Free Weights above.

14. GASTROCNEMIUS (calf)

Free Weights   14a   Stand with your feet 2 feet apart. Hold a barbell across the back of your shoulders (preferably) or a dumbbell on each shoulder. Press up onto the balls of your feet slowly, trying to get as high up as you can. Your knees should be locked throughout. Come back down slowly. Repeat 12 times.

Free Weights   14b   Calf raises. Stand with the balls of your feet on the edge of a step so that your heels are hanging over the step. Hold the handrail slightly for balance, not for a push. Start with your heels as far below the step as they will go. Press up until your heels are as high in the air as they will go. Repeat 25 times. Your knees should be locked throughout.

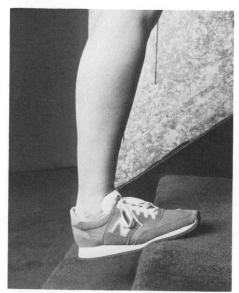 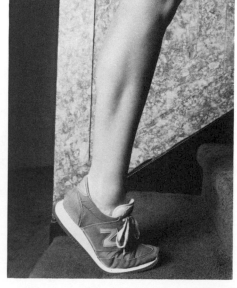

Universal   **14c**   Sit at the leg press station, feet on the lower pedals. Press out slowly until your knees lock. Edge your feet down carefully until only the balls of your feet are on the bottom edge of the pedals. Start with your heels as far away from you as they will go. Press forward with the balls of your feet until your heels are as close to you as they will come.

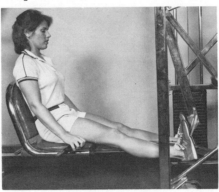 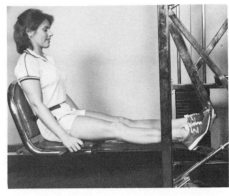

Nautilus   **14d**   Stand on the second step of the omnipurpose machine so that just the balls of your feet are on the edge of the step and your heels are as low below the step as they will go. The belt attached to the weights should be around your waist. Press up until your heels are as high as they will go. Come back down slowly. Your knees should be locked throughout.

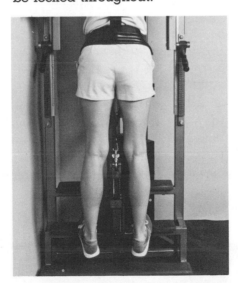 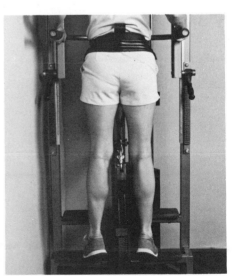

Nautilus   **14e**   If you have access to the Nautilus leg press machine, proceed exactly as outlined under the Universal exercise above (**14c**).

15. ABDOMINALS (all the stomach and sides area)

15a   Leg raises work the upper part of the stomach. This is an isometric exercise where you hold one difficult position for 60 seconds instead of moving throughout the exercise. Lie on your back on a rug or a mat (a hard floor is bad for the back). Make sure a second-hand sweep or a digital second hand is within your vision, either on a clock or your own watch. At the same time that you lift your legs, knees locked, 6 inches off the floor, also lift your back and head 6 inches off the floor. Six inches is the perfect height—any more than this will not work the stomach as well. Only your buttocks should be touching the floor. Hold your arms, relaxed, out to the side for balance. If you can't stay up for 60 seconds at first, do any number of intervals that make up 60 seconds, such as three 20-second intervals with a 10-second rest between each. But eventually, the exercise is to be performed for 60 continuous seconds.

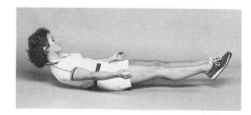

15b   Leg lifts for the lower part of the stomach. Lie on your back on a rug or a mat. Reach behind you and grab someone's ankles, sturdy table legs or part of a machine to keep your upper body down. Keeping your back and head on the ground, lift your legs, knees locked, until they are straight up. Lower them slowly until they come within 6 inches of the ground. Do not touch down between each rep. Point your toes throughout. Fifteen is the minimum number of reps for these leg lifts. Feel free to do more if you can.

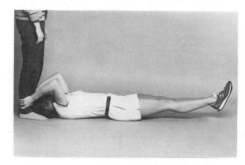

15c   Side bends. You will be surprised what effects this exercise has when it seems so easy. Stand with feet 3 feet apart. Knees locked, lean over to your left side as far as possible, trying to touch your left ankle bone with your left hand. Slowly come back up to the upright position. Then lean to your right side. Do this slowly so that the side muscles really have to pull your torso up each time rather than getting a help from momentum. And do not lean forward during this exercise—then the back pulls you up instead of the sides. Stretch 50 times to each side.

15d   Bent-legged sit-ups. Doing these on a slant board would be best, even if you lower the board to floor level, because you can strap your feet down. In any case, make sure your legs are bent and make sure you do not do these sit-ups on a hard floor. You do not want the vertebrae rolling over a hard surface with no protection. Clasp your hands behind your neck, raise yourself up and touch your chin to either knee, lower yourself until your back just brushes the floor, then raise yourself up again! Do not lower yourself back to the flat-on-the-floor starting position each time. You should do *at least* 25 bent-legged sit-ups to finish up your workout twice a week. If you can do more, more power to you!

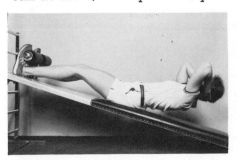 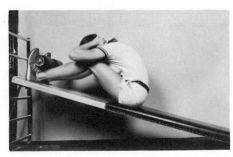

CHAPTER 8

The Advanced Training Manual

Basic Training will not be easy for those of you who are not accustomed to regular, strenuous exercise, but it is an *absolute minimum standard*. If you never go beyond Basic Training, and if it remains a taxing routine for you, you will be fit and healthy. But if it becomes a breeze, and if you decide you want to participate in a competitive sport, then you should progress to Advanced Training.

Advanced Training is for women who have discovered through Basic Training that they have a higher physical potential than they ever imagined. There are eight levels of Advanced Training workouts here, the first being only slightly more difficult and more time-consuming than Basic Training. I have prepared a representative week's worth of sample workouts for each level. Each schedule suggests the time and difficulty of each level—not necessarily the exact workouts to be done week after week if you stay at one level. Each level progresses in difficulty, all the way up to numbers 7 and 8. The only athletes who will find this seventh workout useful are competitive swimmers at a professional or Olympic level, and who spend about 40 or more hours a week training. A minuscule number of you will ever approach these workouts, but you may nevertheless find interesting the ends that some of us will go to while chasing our dreams.

As a point of comparison, I have also made up a high-level racquet-sport player's ideal routine for anyone thinking of giving professional tennis, racquetball, squash or badminton a shot. It's arbitrarily titled Advanced Training Level 8 (for Racquet Sports)—although it is no more advanced or difficult than Level 7. You will see that the dedication of a racquet-sport player must be as intense as that of a swimmer, although the type of training and the number of hours put in do not match. The way in which each spends her time is completely different. And so it would be different for a soccer player, a skier, a basketball player and so on. The workouts for Levels 1 through 5 are for general conditioning, not geared toward any specific sport, although you can use them to better your endurance in any sport you choose. I have indicated at each level what type of goals might be ideal for those workouts. For instance, I consider Level 5 excellent preparation if you are about six months away from running your first marathon. Level 6 is a serious twice-a-day routine for an amateur athlete in the off-season.

For your weight workouts in Advanced Training, you should first do all the Basic Training weight workouts and then add one or more of the advanced variations offered earlier in this manual. All of these advanced variations follow the rules laid down in the introduction to the exercises of the Basic Training Weight-Training Manual for the full description of form. I have arbitrarily assigned Tuesdays and Fridays as weight-lifting days. You may choose any two days as long as you leave 48 hours between weight workouts.

Let's start with these advanced weight-training variations, and then go to the Advanced Training workouts.

1. PUSH-UP VARIATIONS

a. Consult the form for a standard push-up (p. 92), hands at shoulder width. To add some difficulty, you can do 4-count push-ups: Start at the top, elbows locked—that's 1. Lower yourself a quarter of the way to the floor; hold it there 1 full second—that's 2. Lower yourself halfway to the floor; hold it there 1 full second—that's 3. Get down to the bottom position—your whole body 6 inches from the floor; hold 1 full second—that's 4. Come back up to halfway from the floor; hold 1 full second—that's 3. Then three-quarters way from the floor; hold 1 full second—that's 2. Then all the way up, elbows locked—that's 1. So you count 1-2-3-4-3-2-1 from the top position back to the top position. Do 12 push-ups and see how much tougher they are.

b. Push-ups with the hands at shoulder-width position work the chest and the biceps. If you put your hands far out to the sides (first photo), you will work the outsides of the chest near the armpits. These will be easier than regular, shoulder-width push-ups. If you put your hands so that they touch (second photo), you will work the medial line (center of the chest) and the triceps. These will be much harder than regular push-ups.

2. CHINS AND NEGATIVE CHINS

a. Chins, which depend on strong biceps (in relation to body weight), are difficult for women, even strong women. Stand under the chinning bar so that it is directly above your head. Jump up or step up on a stool and grab the bar palms up at shoulder width. Hang so that your elbows are locked; you can either let your legs dangle straight below you or bend them at the knee and cross your ankles behind you or lift your knees in front of you. Pull up until your chin touches the top of the bar. Lower yourself slowly to the elbows-locked position again.

b. For added difficulty, you can do chins palms down instead of palms up. Or you can do them palms up with your hands touching each other instead of at shoulder width.

c. If you can't do any full chins or if you can do some and would like to build up to doing more, do negative chins: Step up on a stool, chair or steps (Nautilus) so that you can easily take a quick hop and touch your chin to the top of the bar. Hold yourself at the top for a count of 5 seconds without touching with your feet for any support. (Imitate this photo.) And still without touching your feet down, lower yourself slowly (to the count of 5 seconds) to the elbows-locked position. Keep your knees bent and your ankles crossed behind you so that your feet won't touch down. Then touch your feet back down and use the stool or chair or steps to push off to get at the top position again. If you do 8 to 10 of these chins every weight workout, they should prepare you to do a few more positive chins (or your first chin-up) on your own eventually.

3. DIPS AND NEGATIVE DIPS

a.   Jump up between the dip bars so that your elbows are locked. Lift your knees in front of you or bend at the knee and cross your ankles behind you. Lower yourself until your chest is at the same level as your hands. Keeping your elbows in close to your body, push back up until your elbows lock again. Dips work your triceps if your body rides up and down vertically during the exercise. If you lean far forward while doing dips, you will also work your chest.

b.   You will be able to do more dips than chins. However, full, deep dips with perfect form are not easy. If you can't do any or you would like to build up to doing more, do negative dips: Push off from a stool or step to easily get into the top, elbows-locked position. Lower yourself slowly (to the count of 5 seconds) until your chest reaches the level of your hands. Keep your knees bent and your ankles crossed behind you so that your feet won't touch down. Then put your feet on the ground and again use a stool or step to easily get back up into the top, elbows-locked position again. Eight to 10 of these negative dips every workout will prepare you to do your first dip or several more positive dips than you were able to do before.

4. ABDOMINALS (general stomach and sides area)

a. Lie on your back on a rug or a mat. Put your calves up on a chair or a stool. Hold a light weight at your chest. Do quick half-sit-ups: Don't come up all the way to your knees like you do for regular sit-ups. Touch your back on the floor each time for just an instant, but always keep your head flexed up. This is one exercise that should be done as quickly as possible. Do 3 sets of 25 reps, 15 seconds between sets.

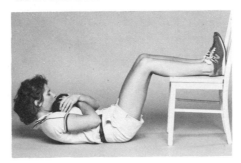 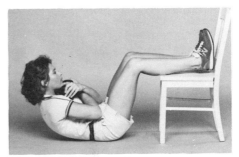

b. Tilt your incline board to the top or near-top position. Bend your knees slightly after you hook your feet under the rollers. Cross your arms over your chest or, if your stomach and lower back are really strong, hold a light weight at your chest. Start with your back 6 inches off the board. Lift up extremely slowly until you are looking straight across the room. Do not come all the way forward to your knees as in regular sit-ups. Lower yourself extremely slowly until you are just 6 inches off the board again. Do not touch down. Do 12 sit-ups this way. "Slowly" is the key to success in this exercise; each sit-up should take as long as 10 seconds if done properly.

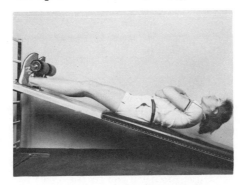 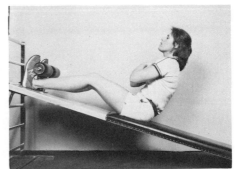

c. Crunches take coordination and balance but are excellent workouts for both the upper and lower stomach muscles. Lie on your back on a rug or a mat. Hook your hands behind your neck. Raise your back 6 inches off the floor and your legs 6 inches off the floor so that only your buttocks are touching down. This is the starting position for crunches. Simultaneously bring your knees in toward your nose and reach your nose out toward your knees. You may have to release your hands to the side to give you balance. Do 12 crunches.

d. Do side bends exactly as described in exercise 15c on p. 125, but hold a light dumbbell in each hand. Thirty reps to each side will really tone your sides and firm up loose flesh around your waist.

e. If you have access to a Roman Chair (described in exercise 1e under the Nautilus system for lower back work on p. 98), you can also work the stomach and sides on this device. For the stomach, lie on your back with your hips just over the edge and your shins under the rollers. Arms crossed on your chest, lean back so that you are looking straight up at the ceiling; then pull yourself up so that you are looking straight across the room. Do 12 of these raises but be sure your lower back is up to it; they are very strenuous. See the first set of photos here. These can also be done holding a light weight at your chest—if your lower back can handle the strain. Then lie on your left side with your hips just over the edge and the sides of your calves under the rollers. With your hands clasped behind your neck, lean over until your left elbow comes as close to the floor as possible. Then come up until you are looking straight across the room. Do 12 reps on your left side, then 12 on your right. See the second set of photos here.

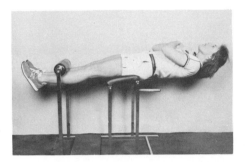 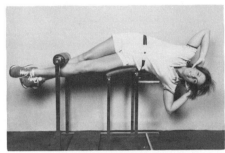 

f.   Use the dip bars. Since most sit-up variations and abdominal exercises are for the upper abdominals, the following would be extremely helpful. Grip the handles of the dip bars with your elbows firmly on the pads, your legs hanging straight down. Slowly lift your knees all the way up to your chest; then slowly let your legs down until they hang straight down again. Do 15 of these. Take a 15-second break and get back into the starting position again. This time lift your legs up together, trying to keep your knees locked and trying to get them high enough so that they are parallel with the floor; then lower them to the starting position. Do 15 of these. Do these slowly, with control; do not swing your legs so that momentum carries them up. Use your stomach to lift them slowly into position. Some weight rooms offer a device for the lower abdominals that looks like a chair without a seat high off the ground. If your gym has this device, proceed as you would on the dip bars.

g. Cross-overs. Lie on your back on a rug or mat. Hands clasped behind your head, back flat on the floor, legs 6 inches off the floor, knees locked. Very rapidly, start crossing your ankles over each other in quick short movements. First cross the right ankle over the left, then the left over the right and continue until each is crossed 25 times. The key to working the stomach in this exercise is keeping your knees locked.

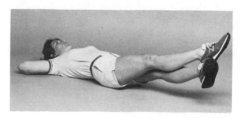

5. TRICEPS

If you have a Universal lat bar or a Nautilus upper torso machine bar, do the exercise described under Universal tricep press (exercise 6c, p. 110), except do it palms up. Use a very light weight. Hook just 2 fingers and your thumb over the bar, thumbs as close together as possible. Keeping your elbows tight in to the body, press down until your elbows are as close to locked as you can get them. As in Basic Training, do not let your hands come up higher than chest height on each rep.

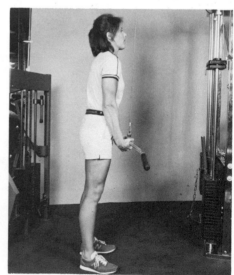

6. BICEPS

a. Do simultaneous curls exactly as described under Free Weights, exercise 7a, p. 111. But now lower the weights in 4 counts, stopping for an instant a quarter of the way down, then half of the way down and finally all the way down. Start at the top, dumbbells touching the shoulders—that's 1. One fourth of the way down is 2. Halfway down is 3. Elbows locked is 4. Halfway back up is 3. Three-quarters of the way back up is 2. All the way up is 1 again. You can do these curls with both Universal and Nautilus, too.

b. Use a weight twice as heavy as the one you do full curls with. Use free weights, Universal or Nautilus. Do short, quick curls at the top of the rep. Never go farther down than the level pictured here.

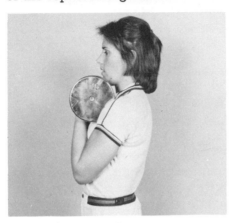 

7. DELTOIDS

a. If you use free weights, refer to lateral raises, exercise 3a (p. 102). These will be front raises. Start with a dumbbell in each hand, each resting on the front of your thighs, palms down. One at a time, elbow slightly bent, raise an arm until it is straight out in front of you. Alternate arms. Keep your body perfectly still throughout—move your arms only.

b. If you use Nautilus, do lateral raises at the deltoid machine. Extend your arms to the side, elbows slightly bent, so that your forearms touch the bottom of the side bars. Simultaneously, press both arms up until they reach shoulder height. Slowly lower them until they come within 2 inches of touching down. Repeat.

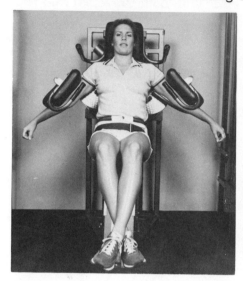 

8. LATS

If you use Universal or Nautilus, perform the lat pull-downs exactly as described in exercises 2c–2f on pp. 100–101, except that now you will pull the bar down in front of you to touch your chest instead of the back of your neck.

 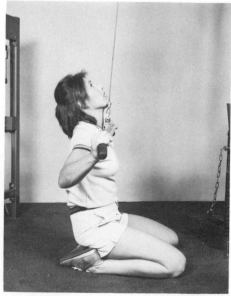

9. QUADRICEPS

a. First of all, you can extend the time of the 90/90's that you do 6 days a week in Basic Training. Try doing reps of 2 minutes of 90/90's followed by 30 seconds of rest for 6, 8 or 10 minutes—or whatever it takes to really burn the quads.

b. On your leg extensions for Universal or Nautilus (described in exercises 9c and 9d on p. 116), try a variation of the 12-rep norm. Let's say 5 plates is ideal for you for 12 tough, achievable reps on the Nautilus leg extension machine. Do the following: 4 reps with 6 plates, 8 reps with 5 plates, and 12 reps with 3 plates. This will build both strength and endurance.

10. BUTTOCKS

a. There is an excellent machine just for the "glutes" (gluteus maximus) made by Digger. You lie on your back, feet on the pedals, with your body as close to the pedals as possible. Squeeze the pedals slowly, stopping just short of a locked-knees position. Then bring both pedals back in as far as you can—the farther you can stretch back, the harder the buttocks will have to work. After 5 or 6 reps with both legs, keep the left leg out while the right leg works in and out. Then keep the right leg out while the left leg works. Alternate until you do 12 reps on each leg. Nautilus makes a new, similar machine for the buttocks.

 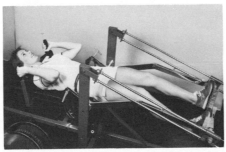 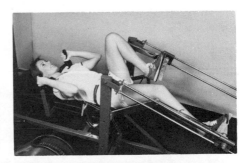

b. Squat down in the leap-frog position, hands clasped behind your neck, up on your toes. Try to leap as far as possible in one direction 10 times. Rest 15 seconds (stand up or sit down) and leap 10 more times. Rest 15 seconds; leap 10 more times. This will also work the quads and the calves but it is extremely strenuous on the knees. Do not do this exercise if you have any knee problems.

c. If you lower the seat on a stationary bike way below your normal height, pedaling will put extra strain on the buttocks. Normal height will mean that your knee will be slightly bent as the pedal is at the very bottom of its revolution; the seat will be low enough to work the buttocks when your knee is very bent at the bottom of the pedal's revolution.

11. PECTORALS

Take one dumbbell and stand with your feet 3 feet apart. Hold the dumbbell with both hands down by your crotch. Your elbows should be locked and your knees slightly bent. Keeping your elbows locked, slowly lift the dumbbell straight out in front of you and up until it is directly over your head. Lower the dumbbell slowly back to the starting position, elbows locked throughout.

12. ADDUCTORS

a. Digger makes an excellent machine especially for the adductors/abductors. Sitting on a rug or mat, spread your legs as far to each side as possible, pads at the inside of the ankles, knees locked. Press in with both legs until the pads touch. Release slowly and try to stretch out to the sides 1 inch farther than where you started. Sit up straight throughout instead of lying down—the upright position is better for your back. The more slowly you can do this exercise, the better results you will have.

b.   Find a place to brace yourself off the ground with your arms—such as the dip bars or the chinning bar. Hold your body still and, with an ankle weight or a weight attached by a strap to your ankle, lift your left knee up until your thigh is parallel to the floor. After you finish 12 reps with the left leg, work the right leg. Doing this exercise without a weight attached to your ankle and bringing your knees up to your chest will be strictly for your abdominals.

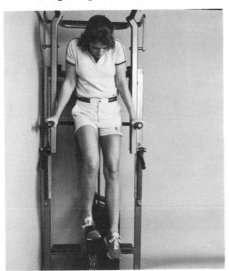 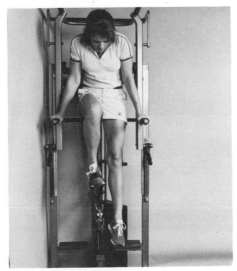

c.   You can extend the time you spend doing the second position of 90/90's (legs spread as wide as possible). Either do all of your required 3 minutes in this second position or continue to do both positions and increase the time for the second. For instance, go 2 minutes in the first position, rest 30 seconds, 2 minutes in the second, rest 30 seconds, and 2 more minutes in the second.

13. ABDUCTORS

a.   Again, use the Digger machine. Sit with both legs straight in front of you, pads at the outside of the ankles, knees locked. Press out with both legs as far as you possibly can. Come back in slowly until your feet touch again. Sit up straight throughout instead of lying on your back. Again, the more slowly you can do this, the better the results.

b.   Refer to exercise 13a. Kneel on the floor, palms down and shoulder width apart. Lift the left knee up until it is as high as your buttocks. Extend your entire left leg so that it is parallel to the floor. Knees locked, do 20 tiny circles forward with your entire left leg. Then do 20 tiny circles backward with the same leg. Repeat, both forward and backward circles with the right leg. This should really burn the outside of the thigh. Do more than 20 each way if your legs aren't burning.

14. LOWER BACK

Do the same lower back lift off the Roman Chair which you did in Basic Training in exercise 1e on p. 98. This time hold a weight with both hands at your chest throughout the movement. This can be extremely strenuous on the lower back. Be careful to warm up well and do these raises very slowly.

15. CALVES

a.   Do the same calf presses on the ground with a barbell across your shoulders as you do in exercise 14a under Free Weights (p. 122). But now, instead of doing 12 reps with toes pointing straight ahead, do 12 with toes pointed way out, 12 with toes pointed straight ahead and 12 very pigeon-toed. These will work the entire contour of the calf.

 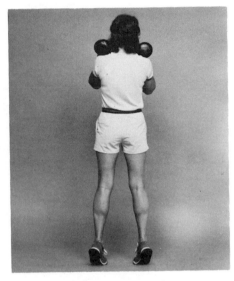

b.   When you do calf presses on the stairs or on the steps of the Nautilus multipurpose machine (see exercise 14d on p. 123), do 12 reps with toes pointed way out, 12 with toes pointed straight ahead and 12 very pigeon-toed.

c.   When you work the calves on the Universal or the Nautilus leg press, do a set of 12 reps with toes pointed way out, 12 with toes pointed straight out and 12 very pigeon-toed (see exercise 14c on p. 123 for original form).

16. FOREARMS

a. There are grip devices available at most sporting goods stores which look like nutcrackers. They come in varying difficulties of tension. Squeeze this device until the handles touch; release all the way before squeezing again. Do 10 reps with the right hand, 10 with the left, until you have completed 50 reps with each hand. Do not waste valuable time at your weight workout doing these; do them riding in the car, watching television and so on. You can do them every day if you especially want to develop your hand, grip, wrist and forearm strength for a racquet sport, rock climbing, *etc*. But don't fall into the habit of only working one hand; you don't want unequal development.

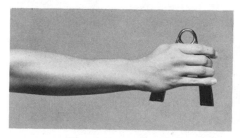 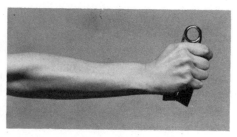

b. Take a double-page sheet of newspaper and crumple it up into a tight wad using your right hand only. Crumple another sheet with your left hand only. Continue until you have crumpled 5 sheets with each hand.

c. Squeeze a tennis or racquet ball as hard as you can with your right hand for 10 continuous seconds. Then squeeze the ball as hard as you can with your left hand for 10 continuous seconds. Continue until you have squeezed hard for 60 seconds total with each hand.

THE WORKOUTS

As in Basic Training, "aerobics" means running, cycling, swimming, skipping rope, rowing or cross-country skiing. Cross-country skiing may be difficult in terms of continuity. For instance, if you are supposed to go 15 continuous minutes at a certain pulse rate, your skill on skis may not allow you to keep up this rate while changing course or winding your way through woods. The same holds true for rowing outside (rather than on an ergometer). The first four exercises lend themselves better to control.

Pay close attention to the time designated for "easy pace" and "rest." If you are supposed to rest 1 minute, this does not mean a minute or two, it means 60 seconds precisely. "Rest" designates stopping movement completely. "Easy pace" designates slowing down to a pace that is barely moving (walking for runners, slow breaststroke for swimmers, easy pedaling for cyclists). The only case where this is not true is skipping rope. If you are doing a skipping workout, stop completely when "easy pace" is indicated.

If I indicate 5 minutes running and you are doing a swimming workout and 5 minutes precisely brings you to the middle of a lap, finish the lap. Use common sense to get as close to 5 minutes (or whatever is called for) as possible. The two important things to remember are: (1) not to do *less* than the time designated for work, and (2) not to take *more* time at rest or at an easy pace than designated. You will be doing quite a bit of Fartlek training, which is nonstop activity combining slow and fast paces; here especially you should be precise about following the time charts.

It is also imperative that you follow the pulse rate indications precisely. In Basic Training you perform all your aerobic activity at a pulse rate minimum of 80 percent of 220 minus your age. In Advanced Training, there will be many workouts where this pulse rate is still called for. Other workouts call for 60 percent, 70 percent, 90 percent and even 100 percent of 220 minus your age. (For instance, if you are 30 years old and you want to work at 100 percent of 220 minus 30, your pulse should be 190. All these pulse rates are MINIMUM indications and I use them as convenient guidelines. If I were coaching you as an individual and knew your skills as a runner or swimmer I would say "run five 440's at an 80-second pace on a 2-minute interval," or "swim five 100-meter freestyles at a 1:10 pace on a 1:30 interval." But as I am coaching you as a group and don't know your individual level of ability or even which exercise you will be performing, I have used pulse rate to indicate your intensity. Your age is taken into account in the formula "220 minus your age"; such other individual differences as skill or strength do not matter for general conditioning guidelines—work at the pulse rate asked of you. Also, do what the workout calls for. If I ask you to do five 1-minute sprints at 90 percent of 220 minus your age with 15 seconds rest between each, don't assume that 5 continuous minutes will be the same. All the workouts at every level are carefully designed to combine a specific ratio of Long Slow Distance ("LSD" in marathon circles) to 80 percent-effort middle distance to near-maximum short work.

ADVANCED TRAINING: LEVEL 1

Level 1 is not a great deal more difficult than Basic Training. You may not have much past experience with sports or strenuous exercise but you have conquered Basic Training over an extended period of time and now you want to spend just a little extra time and effort on your body. The key difference is that you will work shorter periods at a higher pulse rate along with your 15 continuous minutes at a pulse rate of 80 percent of 220 minus your age.

MONDAY

Stretch 5 min. (30 sec. at each position, pp. 67–77).
Warm-up 2 min. to a pulse rate of at least 100.
Aerobics 10 min. (80% of 220 minus age); easy pace 3 min.
Aerobics 10 min. (80%).
Stretch 5 min. (again 30 sec. at each position).
90/90's 3 min.

Total: 38 min.

TUESDAY

Stretch 5 min. (30 sec. at each position, pp. 67–77).
Warm-up 2 min. to a pulse rate of at least 100.
Aerobics 5 min. (80% of 220 minus age); rest 30 sec.
Aerobics 5 min. (90%); rest 30 sec.
Aerobics 5 min. (80%); rest 30 sec.
Aerobics 5 min. (90%); rest 30 sec.

Aerobics 5 min. (80%).
Stretch 5 min. (again 30 sec. at each position).
90/90's 3 min.
Approximately 30 min. weight work.

Total: 1 hr., 12 min.

WEDNESDAY

Stretch 5 min. (30 sec. at each position, pp. 67–77).
Warm-up 2 min. to a pulse rate of at least 100.
Aerobics 10 min. (80% of 220 minus age); easy pace 2 min.
Aerobics 10 min. (80%).
Stretch 5 min. (again 30 sec. at each position).
90/90's 3 min.

Total: 37 min.

THURSDAY

Stretch 5 min. (30 sec. at each position, pp. 67–77).
Warm-up 2 min. to a pulse rate of at least 100.
Aerobics 10 min. (80% of 220 minus age); rest 1 min.
Aerobics 2 min. (100%); rest 1 min.
Aerobics 2 min. (100%); rest 1 min.
Aerobics 2 min. (100%); rest 1 min.
Aerobics 2 min. (100%).
Stretch 5 min. (again 30 sec. at each position).
90/90's 3 min.

Total: 37 min.

FRIDAY

Stretch 5 min. (30 sec. at each position, pp. 67–77).
Warm-up 2 min. to a pulse rate of at least 100.
Aerobics 15 min. (80% of 220 minus age); easy pace 2 min.
Aerobics 5 min. (80%).
Stretch 5 min. (30 sec. at each position).
90/90's 3 min.
Approximately 30 min. weight work.

Total: 1 hr., 7 min.

SATURDAY

Stretch 5 min. (30 sec. at each position, pp. 67–77).
Warm-up 2 min. to a pulse rate of at least 100.
Aerobics 15 min. (80% of 220 minus age); easy pace 1 min.
Aerobics 5 min. (80%).
Stretch 5 min. (again 30 sec. at each position).
90/90's 3 min.

Total: 36 min.

SUNDAY

Rest Day

TOTAL FOR THE WEEK:
4 hrs., 53 min.
(or an average of 42 min. a day for six days with one complete day of rest)

ADVANCED TRAINING: LEVEL 2

Level 2 represents an excellent stage of fitness for anyone of any age. The big step forward at this level is moving up the continuous aerobic time from 15 to 20 minutes. These workouts might better the performance of athletes in sports where cardiovascular conditioning is not a major prerequisite but where mental pressure is very high—like golf or car racing.

MONDAY

Stretch 5 min. (30 sec. at each position, pp. 67–77).
Warm-up 2 min. to a pulse rate of at least 100.
Aerobics 15 min. (80% of 220 minus age); easy pace 3 min.
Aerobics 15 min. (80%).
Stretch 5 min. (again 30 sec. at each position).
90/90's 3 min.

Total: 48 min.

TUESDAY

Stretch 5 min. (30 sec. at each position, pp. 67–77).
Warm-up 2 min. to a pulse rate of at least 100.
Aerobics 15 min. (80% of 220 minus age); rest 3 min.
Aerobics 5 min. (90%); rest 3 min.
Aerobics 5 min. (90%).
Stretch 5 min. (again 30 sec. at each position).
90/90's 3 min.

Approximately 30 min. of weight work.

Total: 1 hr., 16 min.

WEDNESDAY

Stretch 5 min. (30 sec. at each position, pp. 67–77).
Warm-up 2 min. to a pulse rate of at least 100.
Aerobics 15 min. (80% of 220 minus age); rest 1 min.
Aerobics 10 min. (80%); rest 1 min.
Aerobics 5 min. (90%).
Stretch 5 min. (again 30 sec. at each position).
90/90's 3 min.

Total: 47 min.

THURSDAY

Stretch 5 min. (30 sec. at each position, pp. 67–77).
Warm-up 2 min. to a pulse rate of at least 100.
Aerobics 15 min. (80% of 220 minus age); rest 1 min.
Aerobics 5 min. (80%); rest 1 min.
Aerobics 3 min. (90%); rest 1 min.
Aerobics 2 min. (90%).
Stretch 5 min. (again 30 sec. at each position).
90/90's 3 min.

Total: 43 min.

FRIDAY

Stretch 5 min. (30 sec. at each position, pp. 67–77).

Warm-up 2 min. to a pulse rate of at least 100.
Aerobics 20 min. (80% of 220 minus age); easy pace 3 min.
Aerobics 5 min. (80%); rest 2 min.
Aerobics 2 min. (90%) with 15 sec. rest; repeat 5 times.
Stretch 5 min. (again 30 sec. at each position).
90/90's 3 min.
Approximately 30 min. of weight work.

Total: 1 hr., 26 min.

SATURDAY

Stretch 5 min. (30 sec. at each position, pp. 67–77).
Warm-up 2 min. to a pulse rate of at least 100.
Aerobics 20 min. (80% of 220 minus age); easy pace 2 min.
Aerobics 10 min. (80%).
Stretch 5 min. (again 30 sec. at each position).
90/90's 3 min.

Total: 47 min.

SUNDAY

Rest Day

TOTAL FOR THE WEEK:
5 hrs., 46 min.
(or an average of 49 min. a day for six days and one complete day of rest)

ADVANCED TRAINING: LEVEL 3

With Level 3, two long stretches of aerobic work are sandwiched into each daily workout. By this stage you are making a time commitment of nearly an hour a day—and more on weight-training days. These workouts, combined with ball handling training and strategy work, would serve as the perfect type of off-season conditioning for basketball and volleyball players. There is enough continuous work to prepare you for the fast game pace but no workout is overdistanced to detract from your speed.

MONDAY

Stretch 5 min. (30 sec. at each position, pp. 67–77).
Warm-up 2 min. to a pulse rate of at least 100.
Aerobics 20 min. (80% of 220 minus age); easy pace 3 min.
Aerobics 15 min. (80%).
Stretch 5 min. (again 30 sec. at each position).
90/90's 3 min.

Total: 53 min.

TUESDAY

Stretch 5 min. (30 sec. at each position, pp. 67–77).
Warm-up 2 min. to a pulse rate of at least 100.
Aerobics 20 min. (80% of 220 minus age); easy pace 2 min.
Aerobics 3 min. (90%) with 1 min. rest; repeat 5 times.

Stretch 5 min. (again 30 sec. at each position).
90/90's 3 min.
Approximately 30 min. of weight work.

Total: 1 hr., 26 min.

WEDNESDAY

Stretch 5 min. (30 sec. at each position, pp. 67–77).
Warm-up 2 min. to a pulse rate of at least 100.
Aerobics 25 min. (70% of 220 minus age); easy pace 3 min.
Aerobics 5 min. (80%); easy pace 3 min.
Aerobics 10 min. (80%).
Stretch 5 min. (again 30 sec. at each position).
90/90's 3 min.

Total: 1 hr., 1 min.

THURSDAY

Stretch 5 min. (30 sec. at each position, pp. 67–77).
Warm-up 2 min. to a pulse rate of at least 100.
Aerobics 25 min. (80% of 220 minus age); easy pace 5 min.
Aerobics 2 min. (90%) with 15 sec. rest; repeat 5 times.
Stretch 5 min. (again 30 sec. at each position).
90/90's 3 min.

Total: 56 min.

FRIDAY

Stretch 5 min. (30 sec. at each position, pp. 67–77).
Warm-up 2 min. to a pulse rate of at least 100.
Aerobics 25 min. (80% of 220 minus age); easy pace 3 min.
Aerobics 1 min. (100%) with 15 sec. rest; repeat 5 times.
Aerobics 15 min. (70%).
Stretch 5 min. (again 30 sec. at each position).
90/90's 3 min.
Approximately 30 min. of weight work.

Total: 1 hr., 36 min.

SATURDAY

Stretch 5 min. (30 sec. at each position, pp. 67–77).
Warm-up 2 min. to a pulse rate of at least 100.
Aerobics 25 min. (80% of 220 minus age); easy pace 3 min.
Aerobics 15 min. (80%).
Stretch 5 min. (again 30 sec. at each position).
90/90's 3 min.

Total: 58 min.

SUNDAY

Rest Day

TOTAL FOR THE WEEK:
6 hrs., 52 min.
(or an average of 59 min. a day for six days with one complete day of rest)

ADVANCED TRAINING: LEVEL 4

If you are completing Level 4 comfortably, you have proven that you have the discipline to stick with the difficulty of Advanced Training over the long haul. No workout at this level is easy. This would be an ideal conditioning program for a competitive soccer player because there is long enough distance work to prepare you for continuous running—and there is enough high intensity speed work to keep you sharp for the quick sprints required on both offense and defense.

MONDAY

Stretch 5 min. (30 sec. at each position, pp. 67–77).
Warm-up 2 min. to a pulse rate of at least 100.
Aerobics 20 min. (80% of 220 minus age); easy pace 5 min.
Aerobics 20 min. (80%).
Stretch 5 min. (again 30 sec. at each position).
90/90's 3 min.

Total: 1 hr.

TUESDAY

Stretch 5 min. (30 sec. at each position, pp. 67–77).
Warm-up 2 min. to a pulse rate of at least 100.
Aerobics 20 min. (70% of 220 minus age); easy pace 5 min.
Aerobics 20 min. (80%); easy pace 3 min.

Aerobics 3 min. (90%) with 30 sec. rest; repeat 3 times.
Stretch 5 min. (again 30 sec. at each position).
90/90's 3 min.
Approximately 30 min. of weight work.

Total: 1 hr., 43 min.

WEDNESDAY

Stretch 5 min. (30 sec. at each position, pp. 67–77).
Warm-up 2 min. to a pulse rate of at least 100.
Aerobics 25 min. (80% of 220 minus age); easy pace 5 min.
Aerobics 20 min. (80%).
Stretch 5 min. (again 30 sec. at each position).
90/90's 3 min.

Total: 1 hr., 5 min.

THURSDAY

Stretch 5 min. (30 sec. at each position, pp. 67–77).
Warm-up 2 min. to a pulse rate of at least 100.
Aerobics 25 min. (70% of 220 minus age); easy pace 2 min.
Aerobics 5 min. (80%) with 1 min. rest; repeat 4 times.
Stretch 5 min. (again 30 sec. at each position).
90/90's 3 min.

Total: 1 hr., 5 min.

FRIDAY

Stretch 5 min. (30 sec. at each position, pp. 67–77).
Warm-up 2 min. to a pulse rate of at least 100.
Aerobics 30 min. (80% of 220 minus age); easy pace 5 min.
Aerobics 2 min. (90%) with 15 sec. rest; repeat 5 times.
Stretch 5 min. (again 30 sec. at each position).
90/90's 3 min.
Approximately 30 min. of weight work.

Total: 1 hr., 31 min.

SATURDAY

Stretch 5 min. (30 sec. at each position, pp. 67–77).
Warm-up 2 min. to a pulse rate of at least 100.
Aerobics 35 min. (70% of 220 minus age); easy pace 5 min.
Aerobics 10 min. (80%).
Stretch 5 min. (again 30 sec. at each position).
90/90's 3 min.

Total: 1 hr., 5 min.

SUNDAY

Rest Day

TOTAL FOR THE WEEK:
7 hrs., 29 min.
(or an average of 1 hr., 4 min. a day for six days with one complete day of rest)

ADVANCED TRAINING: LEVEL 5

If you are performing more than a continuous hour of aerobic exercise (fast/slow combined) a day, consider yourself a trained athlete. Level 5—six days a week—would probably be too taxing for most athletes in most sports. If you are planning to run your first marathon, this level would provide excellent training for the long distance work of the final 6 months.

MONDAY

Stretch 5 min. (30 sec. at each position, pp. 67–77).
Warm-up 2 min. to a pulse rate of at least 100.
Aerobics 20 min. (80% of 220 minus age); easy pace 3 min.
Aerobics 20 min. (80%); easy pace 3 min.
Aerobics 20 min. (80%).
Stretch 5 min. (again 30 sec. at each position).
90/90's 3 min.

Total: 1 hr., 21 min.

TUESDAY

Stretch 5 min. (30 sec. at each position, pp. 67–77).
Warm-up 2 min. to a pulse rate of at least 100.
Aerobics 20 min. (70% of 220 minus age); easy pace 5 min.
Aerobics 20 min. (80%); easy pace 5 min.
Aerobics 3 min. (90%) with 1 min. rest; repeat 5 times.
90/90's 3 min.
Approximately 30 min. weight work.

Total: 1 hr., 54 min.

WEDNESDAY

Stretch 5 min. (30 sec. at each position, pp. 67–77).
Warm-up 2 min. to a pulse rate of at least 100.
Aerobics 30 min. (80% of 220 minus age); easy pace 5 min.
Aerobics 15 min. (80%); easy pace 5 min.
Aerobics 15 min. (80%).
Stretch 5 min. (again 30 sec. at each position).
90/90's 3 min.

Total: 1 hr., 25 min.

THURSDAY

Stretch 5 min. (30 sec. at each position, pp. 67–77).
Warm-up 2 min. to a pulse rate of at least 100.
Aerobics 25 min. (70% of 220 minus age); easy pace 3 min.
Aerobics 10 min. (80% of 220 minus age); easy pace 3 min.
Aerobics 1 min. (90%) with 15 sec. rest; repeat 5 times.
Rest 2 min.
Aerobics 30 sec. (100%) with 30 sec. rest; repeat 10 times.
Stretch 5 min. (again 30 sec. at each position).
90/90's 3 min.

Total: 1 hr., 12 min.

FRIDAY

Stretch 5 min. (30 sec. at each position, pp. 67–77).
Warm-up 2 min. to a pulse rate of at least 100.
Aerobics 30 min. (80% of 220 minus age); easy pace 5 min.
Aerobics 20 min. (80%); easy pace 5 min.
Aerobics 15 min. (80%).
Stretch 5 min. (again 30 sec. at each position).
90/90's 3 min.
Approximately 30 min. of weight work.

Total: 2 hrs.

SATURDAY

Stretch 5 min. (30 sec. at each position, pp. 67–77).
Warm-up 2 min. to a pulse rate of at least 100.
Aerobics 7 min. (90%); rest 30 sec.
Aerobics 8 min. (90%); rest 45 sec.
Aerobics 9 min. (90%); rest 1 min.
Aerobics 10 min. (80%); rest 1 min.
Aerobics 9 min. (80%); rest 45 sec.
Aerobics 8 min. (90%); rest 30 sec.
Aerobics 7 min. (90%).
Stretch 5 min. (again 30 sec. at each position).
90/90's 3 min.

Total: 1 hr., 17 min.

SUNDAY

Rest Day

TOTAL FOR THE WEEK:
9 hrs., 14 min.
(or an average of 1 hr., 19 min. a day six days a week with one complete day of rest)

ADVANCED TRAINING: LEVEL 6

If you are only interested in general conditioning and you have come to Level 6, you have come too far. This much training, twice a day, is geared toward performance—for an experienced marathon runner, for example, who wants to develop some speed—or for a college basketball player who has decided to work during the summer to improve her conditioning. These workouts will give you an idea of how difficult it is for an amateur athlete to hold a full-time job and put in this kind of time and energy before and after work.

MONDAY

A.M. Stretch 5 min. (30 sec. at each position, pp. 67–77). Warm-up 2 min. to a pulse rate of at least 100. Aerobics 45 min. (80% of 220 minus age); easy pace 5 min. Aerobics 10 min. (80%). Stretch 5 min. (30 sec. at each position).

P.M. Aerobics 5 min. (80%) with 1 min. easy pace; repeat 10 times. Stretch 5 min. (30 sec. at each position). 90/90's 3 min.

Total: 2 hrs., 20 min.

TUESDAY

A.M. Stretch 5 min. (30 sec. at each position, pp. 67–77). Warm-up 2 min. to a pulse rate of at least 100. Aerobics 45 min. (60% of 220 minus age); easy pace 5 min. Aerobics 5 min. (80%). Stretch 5 min. (30 sec. at each position).

P.M. Aerobics 20 min. (60%). Aerobics 1 min., 2 min., 3 min., 4 min., 5 min., 5 min., 4 min., 3 min., 2 min., 1 min. (90%) with 1 min. easy pace between each. Stretch 5 min. (30 sec. at each position). 90/90's 3 min. Approximately 30 min. of weight work.

Total: 2 hrs., 45 min.

WEDNESDAY

A.M. Stretch 5 min. (30 sec. at each position, pp. 67–77). Warm-up 2 min. to a pulse rate of at least 100. Aerobics 20 min. (00% of 220 minus age); easy pace 3 min. Aerobics 20 min. (80%); easy pace 3 min. Aerobics 20 min. (80%).

P.M. Aerobics 5 min. (80%) with 1 min. easy pace; repeat 12 times. Stretch 5 min. (30 sec. at each position). 90/90's 3 min.

Total: 2 hrs., 32 min.

THURSDAY

A.M. Stretch 5 min. (30 sec. at each position, pp. 67–77). Warm-up 2 min. to a pulse rate of at least 100. Aerobics 25 min. (80% of 220 minus age); easy pace 5 min. Aerobics 20 min. (80%). Stretch 5 min. (30 sec. at each position). Aerobics 30 min. (crescendo starting very slowly, just over a walk with a pulse of about 90 and up the pace every 5 min. so that that last 5 min. is very fast at 90% of 220 minus your age).

P.M. No rest. Aerobics 30 min. (60%). Stretch 5 min. (30 sec. at each position). 90/90's 3 min.

Total: 2 hrs., 10 min.

FRIDAY

A.M. Stretch 5 min. (30 sec. at each position, pp. 67–77). Warm-up 2 min. to a pulse rate of at least 100. Aerobics 50 min. (80% of 220 minus age); easy pace 5 min. Aerobics 10 min. (80%). Stretch 5 min. (30 sec. at each position).

(continued on next page)

P.M. Aerobics 2 min. (90%) with 30 sec. rest; repeat 30 times.
Stretch 5 min. (30 sec. at each position).
90/90's 3 min.
Approximately 30 min. of weight work.

Total: 3 hrs., 10 min.

SATURDAY

Stretch 5 min. (30 sec. at each position, pp. 67–77).
Aerobics 55 min. (80% of 220 minus age).
Stretch 5 min. (30 sec. at each position).

Total: 1 hr., 5 min.

SUNDAY

Rest Day

TOTAL FOR THE WEEK: 14 hrs., 11 min.
(or an average of 2 hrs., 1 min. a day six days a week with one complete day of rest)

ADVANCED TRAINING: LEVEL 7 (for Swimming)

At this sophisticated level of training, swimmers and runners or other aerobic sport athletes do not train alike. If you are training for the Boston Marathon, you cannot simply slip "running" into this schedule every time "swimming" is called for. I would follow this schedule some time in the middle of my year of training for a major swim. This week would occur after I have gotten in pretty good shape but long before I am swimming eight hours a day—and swimming only—during the final few months. Note that these swimming workout routines do not include 90/90's—there is plenty of leg work already with running, skipping and stationary bike work.

MONDAY

A.M. Stretch 5 min.
Run 10 miles on ¼-mile track—shoot for 60–65 min.
Stretch 5 min.

NOON Skip rope 10 min.; rest 1 min.
Skip rope 10 min.; rest 1 min.
Skip rope 10 min.; rest 1 min.
Skip rope 10 min.; rest 1 min.
Skip rope 10 min.

P.M. Stretch 5 min.
Swim 4 hrs. at a 50-meter pool—2 hrs. of 1000-, 500-, 400-, 200-, 100-meter intervals of all different combinations at 80% of 220 minus-age pulse rate; 2 hrs. of continuous swimming at 70% or 220 minus-age pulse rate.

Total: 6 hrs., 9 min.

TUESDAY

A.M. Stretch 5 min.
Run 7 miles in 45 min. on ¼-mile track; rest 5 min.;

run 12 1-min. sprints with 30-sec. walk between each.
Stretch 5 min.

NOON Skip rope 15 min.; rest 2 min.
Skip rope 15 min.; rest 2 min.
Skip rope 15 min.
Work the speed bag for 5 continuous min.

P.M. Approximately 30 min. of weight work
Stretch 5 min.
Swim 3 hrs. continuously in the ocean at about 2.2 mph.

Total: 5 hrs., 38 min.

WEDNESDAY

A.M. Stretch 5 min.
Run 10 miles on ¼-mile track in 70 min.
Stretch 5 min.

NOON Skip rope 30 min.; rest 5 min.
Skip rope 10 min.
Do 1-min. sprints on the stationary bike with 15 sec. rest; repeat 10 times.

P.M. Stretch 5 min.
Swim 4 hrs. in a 50-meter pool—8 repeat 1500-meter swims on the half hour, resting or slow stretching swimming for the minutes in between each.

Total: 6 hrs., 13 min.

THURSDAY

A.M. Stretch 5 min.
Run 7 miles in 45 min. on ¼-mile track; rest 5 min.; run 8 1-min. sprints with 30-sec. walk between each; run 8 30-sec. sprints with 30-sec. walk between each.
Stretch 5 min.

NOON Skip rope 20 min.; rest 3 min.
Skip rope 20 min.; rest 3 min.
Skip rope 20 min.
Work the speed bag for 10 continuous min.

P.M. Stretch 5 min.
Swim 3 hrs. continuously in the ocean, trying to step up the pace each hour.

Total: 5 hrs., 41 min.

FRIDAY

A.M. Stretch 5 min.
Run 10 miles on ¼-mile track—shoot for 60 min.; no rest; jog 15 min. at easy pace (8½- to 9-min. miles).
Stretch 5 min.

NOON Skip rope 30 min.; rest 5 min.
Skip rope 30 min.
Do 30-sec. sprints on the stationary bike with 10 sec. rest; repeat 10 times.

P.M. Approximately 30 min. of weight work.
Stretch 5 min.
Swim 4 hrs. at a 50-meter pool—1 hr., 400's with 1 min. rest between each; 1 hr. 200's with 30 sec. rest between each; 1 hr. 100's with 20 sec. rest between each; 1 hr. 50's with 15 sec. rest between each.

Total: 7 hrs., 6 min.

SATURDAY

A.M. Stretch 5 min.
Run 10 miles in 75 min. on ¼-mile track.
Stretch 5 min.

NOON Skip rope 45 min.; rest 5 min.
Skip rope 15 min.

P.M. Stretch 5 min.
Swim 4 hrs. continuously in the ocean shooting for distance; I do this each Saturday to try to get farther down the coast in the same time each week.

Total: 6 hrs., 35 min.

SUNDAY

Stretch 30 min. in a whirlpool bath or very hot bath at home; get a 1-hr. massage if possible.
Stretch 30 min. after the bath.

Total: 1 hr.

TOTAL FOR THE WEEK:
38 hrs., 22 min.
(or an average of 5 hrs., 28 min. a day)

ADVANCED TRAINING: LEVEL 8 (for Racquet Sports)

Obviously, a tennis player has to work on different skills than a squash or racquetball or badminton or table tennis player. "Racquet work" here indicates all the strokes, shots, spins, serves, strategy, match play and so on that you should study and perfect for each specific racquet sport. This week is appropriate for a player getting ready for the competitive season, not someone already in tournament play.

MONDAY

A.M.   Stretch 5 min.
2 hrs. racquet work.
30 min. skipping rope—sprint 1 min., rest 15 sec., repeat.
6 min. 90/90's (3 min. in each position).
Stretch 5 min.

P.M.   Stretch 5 min.
2 hrs. racquet work.
Run 8 440's (at 90% of 220 minus your age pulse rate) on track with 1 min. between each.
Stretch 5 min.

Total: 5 hrs., 15 min.

TUESDAY

A.M.   Stretch 5 min.
2 hrs. racquet work.
20 min. skipping rope—sprint 2 min., rest 30 sec., repeat.
5 min. court sprints—sprint 1 min. around court, simulating movement of game but without ball, rest 30 sec., repeat—keep low on the balls of your feet, and take a swing as if you were in a game every few seconds.
Stretch 5 min.

P.M.   2 hrs. racquet work.
Approximately 30 min. weight work, extra work on grip and forearm.
Do 1-min. sprints on the stationary bike with 30 sec. rest (pulse should be at least 180); repeat 5 times.
Stretch 5 min.

Total: 5 hrs., 20 min.

WEDNESDAY

A.M.   Stretch 5 min.
2 hrs. racquet work
30 min. skipping rope—sprint 30 sec., rest 10 sec., repeat.
6 min. 90/90's (3 min. in each position).
Stretch 5 min.

P.M.   2 hrs. racquet work.
Sprint 12 220's on track; walk 220 between each.
Stretch 5 min.

Total: 5 hrs., 20 min.

THURSDAY

A.M.   Stretch 5 min.
2 hrs. racquet work.
15 min. continuous skipping rope.
10 30-sec. court sprints with 20 sec. between each (either straight up and down the court or quick stops and sudden changes in direction covering all of the court).
Stretch 5 min.

P.M.   2 hrs. racquet work.
Run 3 continuous miles at about 8 min./mile.
Stretch 5 min.

Total: 5 hrs., 5 min.

FRIDAY

A.M. Stretch 5 min.
2 hrs. racquet work.
30 min. skipping rope—
sprint 1 min., rest 15 sec.,
repeat.
6 min. 90/90's (3 min. in
each position).
Stretch 5 min.

P.M. 2 hrs. racquet work.
Approximately 30 min.
weight work; extra work
on grip and forearm.
Do 30-sec. sprints on the
stationary bike with 30
sec. rest (pulse should be
at least 180); repeat 10
times.
Stretch 5 min.

Total: 5 hrs., 35 min.

SATURDAY

Stretch 30 min. in whirl-
pool bath or very hot bath
at home.
Stretch 30 min. after your
bath; get a 1-hr. massage
if possible.

Total: 1 hr. (2 hrs. with massage)

SUNDAY

Stretch 5 min.
Play a hard match.
Stretch 30 min.

Total: 2 hrs., 30 min.

**TOTAL FOR THE WEEK:
30 hrs., 5 min.**
(or an average of 4 hrs., 18 min.
a day)

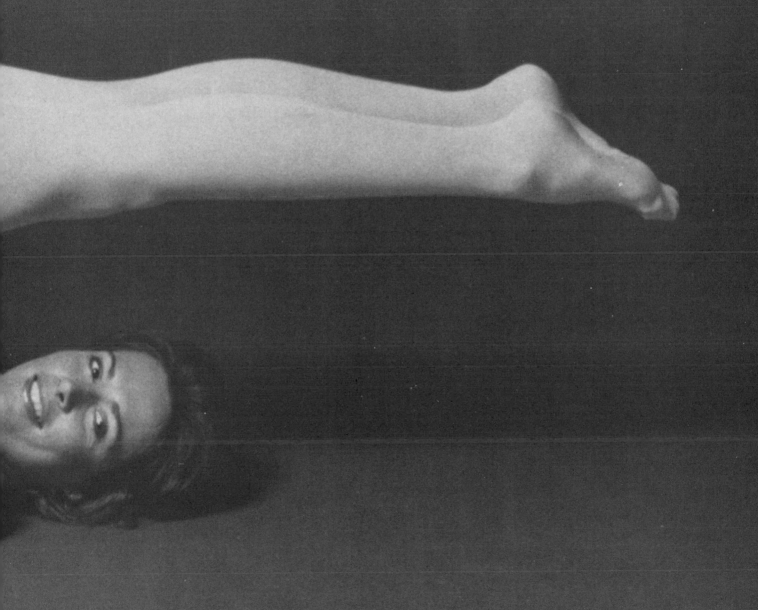

PART IV
THE PRIMERS

CHAPTER 9

Inside Tips

What might you run up against in your adventurous transition from a sedentary condition to a life of robust physical activity? You'll probably never be injured doing Basic Training, but there are simple situations you might confront—such as a turned ankle or 110-degree heat. I want you to know what to do about them so you won't allow easily resolved problems to throw you off stride.

Just remember two basic rules of thumb, regardless of the situation. First, trust your instincts. The more physically active you become, the closer you'll get to sensing what your instincts (and not just your former habits and fears) are telling you. You'll come to know your body and its idiosyncrasies. You will become the best judge of what you can and cannot do. Someone else's opinion will await you around every turn in the track—advice is one of the few things left in life that is free. To chat and commiserate can sometimes be delightful, and you may pick up some useful and entertaining tips. I remember learning, in this way, that "shoe loops" are loops in the tongue of some sneakers through which you thread your shoelaces to keep the tongue from moving, thereby keeping the top of your foot padded; and that a *hydrocolater* is a moist heating pad available in various contours, for the neck, the foot or whatever. But for important things, such as the prevention and treatment of injury or heat exhaustion, hearsay can be useless and even dangerous.

No other athlete or fitness buff knows *your* body, how it moves and what it can handle, better than you. Trust yourself and trust your body. Listen to what it tells you. Much of the time it will even tell you exactly what you need to eat. If you need salt, you'll crave salty foods; if your body lacks potassium, the taste of a banana will be the only thing on your mind; and whenever you really *need* to stop, sharp sudden pain will tell you to, probably in plenty of time to prevent serious injury.

The second rule of thumb is this: If you have any doubt, if your instincts tell you to seek another opinion about an unfamiliar sensation, consult a doctor—preferably one versed in sports medicine—who has a healthy respect for women. I can give you a few sensible tips here, but you will learn almost everything else from experience. The few remaining unknowns lie in the realm of the qualified sports physician. A nonsports-oriented doctor will usually give you the following logic: "Of course you hurt; you're running three miles a day! Stop running, take this pill and the pain will go away." We want a doctor who will help you have your cake and eat it too—who will find the ticket to resolve your pain (without drugs) and allow you to continue to work out at the same time.

Injuries

How to Prevent Injury

You need not bring an untoward fear of injury or of pain with you to Basic Training. Ultimately, even if you should injure yourself, which is not likely, it probably won't be serious or debilitating. Most injuries heal quickly, and, especially if you follow the designated treatment, you will recover and be back in action in the shortest possible time. Most important, you can protect yourself against injury by always warming up by stretching *and* warming down after your workout by stretching again.

You can prevent injury by recognizing when bad pain is warning you of it. Bad pain feels localized, sharp and sudden—you could put your finger right on the spot within a few centimeters. Bad pain signals impending or already occurring injury (except when it is a "stitch" or a muscle cramp, see page 163). When you feel sudden sharp pain in any limb, stop moving it immediately. If you continue to move the area, you risk injuring the painful area more seriously. If it's just a slight twinge of sharp pain, stop and rest for a few minutes. Then begin again more slowly, in this way testing out the first message to see if it really meant something. If the pain recurs, then stop the workout of that part of your body and continue with the rest if possible. If your initial pain continues, proceed to immediate treatment (see page 162).

If the bad pain doesn't come again after you start up, you can assume that the first and only flicker of it was just a flash in the pan, and proceed with your workout. Be especially aware of where you felt it so that if it recurs during the workout, you can treat it as a full-fledged signal (and not just one of those things); but don't focus on it too much or worry it to death. The mind is a powerful force—no one knows how powerful—and who's to say that thinking it is in trouble won't actually turn out to make it so? Be aware of the negative possibilities, but concentrate on the positive side. Think of yourself, if you will, as a galloping, hardy Clydesdale instead of a skitterish thoroughbred. You can indulge yourself later—in a hot whirlpool bath or with a glass of papaya/banana juice. Workouts don't work out well for those who pamper every flicker of fear or discomfort.

Stretching, warming up and warming down are the keys to injury prevention. But you can also prevent injury by being aware of any structural abnormalities and muscle imbalances you might have and by using special equipment, shoes or exercises to nullify them. Structural abnormalities, such as

flat feet, too high arches, unequal leg lengths or bow legs, can put extra stress on other parts of your body and make you more vulnerable to injury.

For example, flat feet can put extra stress on the arch, ankle, hip and lower back. To prevent injury, simply wear good athletic shoes that fit your feet the way that gloves fit your hands. Choose for fit yourself and don't be rushed at the store. In extreme cases of flat feet, a podiatrist can make you an orthotic (a special shoe insert made from a cast of your foot), but be sure you really need it before forking over $100 or more. Usually, common arch supports—available in a drugstore for about $10— will do the trick. You can tell if you have flat feet not only by looking at them, but by noticing whether you land far back on your heels when you run (to compensate for excessive rolling inward of the feet). Another possible indication is that the backs of your shoes always wear out first.

Abnormally high arches can also make you vulnerable to injury. Highly arched feet sometimes don't roll inward enough during the footstrike to distribute one's weight evenly throughout the leg. The excess shock can result in stress fractures of the feet and pain along the outside of the knee. To avoid these problems, run on softer ground, never the pavement. Buy shoes with thick soles, and insert arch supports that are soft and pliable.

A discrepancy between the length of your legs doesn't have to be a big problem, but if you're feeling hip or lower back pain, get out your measuring tape. If the distances between the floor and the same spot on the top of each side of your pelvis are unequal by a quarter of an inch or more, this may be creating pressure upon the hip joint of the longer leg as well as some back pain. To prevent tilting of your pelvis owing to unequal leg lengths, you can have the sole and heel of the shorter leg's shoe built up slightly. But don't do this on your own—it is a subtle job that should be left to a podiatrist.

You can easily compensate for bow legs, which may cause lower back pain. Simply perform the exercises for the adductors on page 69 to stretch your iliopsoas muscles, which run from your pelvis to the upper inner part of your thigh.

Muscle imbalances, like structural abnormalities, can make you more susceptible to injury, but this problem is easy to correct through exercise. Simply stretch the stronger muscle and do weight work on the weaker muscle.

For example, when you run, the quadricep (front of the thigh) brings the knee up, and the hamstring (back of the thigh) brings the knee down. The quadricep and the hamstring are called opposing muscles. When opposing muscles are of unequal strength, sometimes the stronger muscle can overpower the weaker one. This imbalance in strength sometimes can cause pulled or torn tendons and fibers in the weaker muscle. Hamstrings are often weaker than quadriceps, which is why pulled hamstrings are one of the most common injuries in athletes and exercisers. The injury is most common in runners or athletes in sports in which running is sudden and quick off the mark. For example, soccer, basketball and field hockey players almost always have quadriceps nearly one and a half times stronger than their hamstrings. In running, the quadricep must work against gravity to raise the knee when you're propelling yourself forward, but in bringing the knee down, the hamstring derives much help from the downward pull of gravity. Since it doesn't have to work as hard as the quadricep, the hamstring doesn't develop as much strength. Interestingly enough, athletes in such sports as cycling, skiing and skating don't injure their hamstrings as often as running athletes because they don't have to straighten their knees fully.

Balancing your muscle strength is one of the most important arguments for a comprehensive and thorough weight-training program.

Another common injury attributable to muscle imbalance is shin splints. Shin splints are also more common in runners, but instead of gravity, it is momentum that contributes to the muscle imbalance. The calf muscles, which pull the forefoot down, have to work harder than the shin muscles, which have the help of momentum in pulling the forefoot up. Working harder, the calves become proportionately stronger than the shins and, in overpowering them, can injure them. This injury, though called shin splints, has nothing to do with bone fractures.

To treat or avoid shin splints, beef up the resistance work on the shin muscles and concentrate for a while on stretching the calf muscles instead of strengthening them. You can strengthen the shins, as basketball players do, by running up stairs. If your shin splints persist, however, rest the lower leg for a couple of weeks. Elevate your leg and apply ice to your shins for twenty to thirty minutes before going to bed.

Even if you don't compensate for slight structural abnormalities and muscle imbalance, you may never pull a muscle or strain a ligament AS LONG AS YOU WARM UP.

Overwork and Overtraining

While I commend and encourage eagerness and competitive spirit, in some rare cases of excess these qualities could lead to injury or termination of involvement entirely. Take it slowly at first; and follow the guidelines outlined earlier in this book, which are designed to show you how to progress to the right workout at the right time for you. The Basic Training workouts have your fine competitive spirit, your eagerness and your individual abilities in mind. Don't be insulted if your first few weeks are pitifully easy, just as you shouldn't worry if they seem ridiculously hard. Basic Training is for life— you will gradually build to the right level of intensity.

Competitive athletes involved in specific training for their own sport in addition to Basic Training may want to watch out for the following signs of overwork and overtraining: headaches, too much weight loss, absence of menstruation, constipation or diarrhea, loss of appetite, swelling of lymph nodes in the groin, armpit, neck, overall sluggishness and frequent colds. If these symptoms persist over a long period of time (and are not just due to a beginner's adjustment period), then take a few days off and rest or go back to your previous workout stage and don't graduate until that stage becomes too easy for you.

How Can You Tell What's Been Injured?

Out of the body's five hundred or so muscles, only about twenty-five are commonly injured in sports and fitness training. Pain signals will help you to locate the affected area and awareness of the most common injuries associated with the activity will allow some degree of self-diagnosis. Injuries of certain body parts are so typical of certain sports that they have acquired common vernacular names like tennis elbow, swimmer's shoulder, runner's knee.

Whenever sharp, sudden or localized pain strikes, stop your workout, sit down, and while applying ice (see Treatment, below), try to gauge the damage. If you have injured a bone, you'll probably know it immediately. Breaks or fractures of the bone are extremely painful.

Muscle injuries are not so clear-cut. However, since muscles are made up of many soft, contractile fibers, a muscle will hurt a lot when moved or touched if it is injured. (This hurt is distinct from mere soreness experienced the day after intense exercise.) Specifically, if the space between two joints over the long bones (such as the area between the hip and knee or between the shoulder and elbow) really hurts badly, you may have strained, pulled or torn a muscle. (A strain is the least painful of the three, a pull is medium painful and a tear will hurt the most.) If the pain is excruciating over that space, suspect a bone injury.

Tendons are tougher and narrower than muscle and not elastic like ligaments. They attach muscles to either bones, ligaments or cartilage and are usually located at the approach to the joints and the tail of the muscle. An injured tendon will feel much like an injured muscle, painful if you move or touch it by pressing on the skin.

Injuries to or around the joints (ankle, shoulder, elbow, knee, hip, wrist) may involve either the joint itself, ligaments or cartilage. If the joint is painful with movement or to the touch, you may have strained, pulled or torn a ligament or cartilage. Ligaments are elastic, somewhat like rubber bands, and attach bone to bone (as in the joints). Cartilage cushions movements of the joints and covers the ends of the long bones of the body.

The muscles are encased in a kind of sheath or long envelope over which are protective membranes, called fasciae. This close-fitting sleeve of membranes gives the muscles something to push against when they contract. Without fasciae to keep the muscles from bulging out on contraction, much of the force of muscle movement would be lost or dissipated. Because fasciae surround muscles and tendons (as well as almost all the tissue of the body) like thin sheets, injuries to them are difficult to diagnose on your own. The most common fascial injury is *plantar fasciitis*—a partial or complete tear of the fascia over the muscles under the foot. Though it can be signaled by pain anywhere on the bottom of the foot, the most common symptom is pain, without swelling, just under the heel bone where one end of the plantar fascia is. (The other end attaches to the toes.) Sometimes caused by sudden turns, shoes without arch support, shoes with very stiff soles or any pressure on the bottom of the foot excessive enough to flatten the arch or spread the toes, the injury can happen suddenly or develop over time.

Immediate Treatment of Injury

When severe pain tells you of injury in no uncertain terms, stop immediately and rest. Continuing to exercise or move the injured part can do nothing but make it worse. Even before you know exactly what has gone wrong, if it's an orthopedic type injury that has not broken the skin, apply ice. In fact, if you remember nothing else at that moment, remember I-C-E because it stands for the three steps of treatment: (1) *I*ce application, (2) *C*ompression of the area, (3) *E*levation of the area.

The more blood that gathers around the injured tissues, the longer the overall healing time. Ice arrests this collection of blood by causing the injured blood vessels to contract. Because direct application of ice cubes or chips makes the skin hurt, put a towel or cloth over the injured part and place the ice pack or cubes over that.

Wrap the ice in place over the area with an elastic bandage or some makeshift tie, firmly but *loosely enough* so that it does not cut off the blood supply to the limb. The firmness of the wrap provides compression, which will limit the swelling. In general, a decrease in swelling is a sign that the injury has begun to heal.

REMEMBER: *Never tie the compression wrap too tightly—it is dangerous to shut off the blood supply.*

Next, elevate the injured part. (Do this first if you have to wait for someone to get the ice.) Raise it and keep it above the level of the heart; if you're lying down, only a few inches above the ground is sufficient. The force of gravity can minimize swelling by draining the excess fluid down away from the injury.

If possible, stay where you are for 3 hours. During that time, follow this schedule: Apply ice for 30 minutes; then take it off for 15 minutes (to allow the blood to recirculate normally and warm the skin) before reapplying it for another 30 minutes, and so on. If you have to move, have someone transport you to your home during a 30-minute segment of the process with the ice wrap still in place and without moving the injured part. The ice procedure can be repeated for up to 24 hours, which may be necessary if the injury is severe. After 48 hours, if there is still swelling and pain at rest, you can apply heat.

Warning: The ice application itself will be somewhat painful; however, if you feel cramping, numbness and excess pain in the injured area, remove the compression wrap immediately. Tying the ice/compression wrap too tightly is dangerous.

You should consult a physician immediately if you think the injury is to a ligament or in some other way a trauma to the joint; if you feel severe pain, which may indicate a broken bone; if pain in a joint or bone persists for over two weeks; if the injury doesn't heal in three weeks' time; if you detect any symptoms of infection—fever, pus, swollen lymph nodes or red streaks; or if you think you ought to for any reason at all.

Muscle Cramps and Stitches

A muscle cramp is simply a twisting of muscle fibers that have become exhausted or tense. Since they will no longer contract, they collapse. A cramp (sometimes referred to as a charley horse) is nothing serious. At worst, it may leave the area sore for a day or two. The best treatment known is massage. Do it for yourself if you're alone, or have someone dig their fingers into the twisted fibers. It will hurt like hell, but you'll have to keep digging until those fibers relax and straighten out again.

A stitch—a muscle cramp of sorts in the diaphragm—is even more harmless. When the fibers compress too tightly to let enough oxygen in, a spot of muscle on your front rib section on either side will blaze in sharp pain. You can try two things. One, raise your arms high in the air and breathe as deeply as possible to force oxygen into your diaphragm. You can even continue to run while you do this, though you must stop for a moment if you're swimming, cycling or skipping rope. Or, without having to stop any exercise, you can try "breathing backward": Suck your diaphragm in hard as you inhale and force it out as you exhale a few times. In any case, a stitch can be annoying and even downright painful, but it is the one exception to the rule of sharp, localized pain: A stitch does not indicate serious injury. People have finished 26-mile marathons after getting a stitch in the first mile and never being able to shake it as they continued!

How to Recover from Injury

I designed Basic Training to minimize your chances of injury during exercise. (You'll even find as you become stronger and more fit through Basic Training that you'll be much less likely to hurt yourself when rearranging the furniture or by stepping into an unseen rut in the sidewalk.) But if you do suffer a chance mishap, remember that most exercise injuries don't have to put you out of commission for very long.

You can rehabilitate most injured muscles and tendons by doing slow, gradual strengthening exercises and using plenty of heat (although ice is the treatment for the first 48 hours). Combining the stretching with heat, in a whirlpool bath, sauna, steam room or bathtub, is best. Exercising in water is also excellent therapy. For example, if you've pulled your biceps muscle, take a light dumbbell—perhaps two pounds—and do biceps curls (refer to page 111 for technique) in a pool or whirlpool or even your bathtub.

In the meantime, if you can't exercise the injured area without pain, do aerobic exercises while you're rehabilitating. Do exercises that don't involve movement of the injured part. For example, if your shoulder is hurt, ride a stationary bike; if you have a knee injury, swim. Or try working out on a punching bag from a seated position. In this way, you can try to maintain your cardiovascular conditioning. Also keep in mind that you don't have to skip your whole weight workout necessarily just because one muscle group is injured. Do everything you can while giving that one area the rest it needs.

How to Train in Extreme Temperatures

Cold Weather Training

What you might run up against in the way of outside forces (like the weather) are just as easy to prepare for as injuries are simple to prevent. The hailstones were as big as quarters one winter day, but that was no reason for the New York Women's Soccer Club to call off their regular practice in Central Park—they played anyway, and hats helped. You can exercise safely in any kind of weather as long as you take certain measures to accommodate yourself to extremes in temperature.

The most important thing to do before exercising in extremely cold temperatures is to dress right. Since muscles in action produce heat, you're going to sweat no matter how cold it is outside. When you stop moving, your muscles stop producing heat, but you're left with perspiration covering your skin and that can make you cold through evaporation, especially if the wind penetrates your clothing. So, in outdoor aerobics and in stop-and-go sports, as any skier knows, avoid hazards of extreme cold (hypothermia and frostbite) by layering your clothing. Air is trapped between each layer, and air is one of the best insulators. You can peel off outer layers when you get too warm or add them as a shield if a wind comes up.

I recommend the following layers of clothing: Polypropylene undershirt, short-sleeved T-shirt, thin cotton turtleneck, sweater (optional, depending upon how cold it is), covered with a parka or windbreaker. Polypropylene is a fairly new synthetic fiber; an undershirt made of it keeps your skin dry by transferring perspiration to the layers above.

Since the head, hands and feet get hit by the cold first, you must wear a hat, mittens and warm socks to lock in the heat which would otherwise dissipate away from the skin surface. A flat knit 100-percent wool hat can keep you from losing as much as 20 percent of your body heat. Mittens are better than gloves because they allow the fingers to warm one another, and down mittens trap the warm air best, especially if you wear silk glove liners. Thin inner socks, such as silk liners or plastic liners (like a sandwich baggie sold in the form of a sock) overlaid with wool socks, will keep your feet dry and warm, but make sure this doesn't interfere with the good fit of your shoes.

Wearing a windbreaker during winter exercise will help you acclimatize faster to exercise in the heat when summer rolls around. Reducing air passage and evaporation, windbreakers make you sweat more so you definitely need a polypropylene undershirt next to the skin if a windbreaker is your outermost layer. Sweating more in the winter will help your body to produce sweat efficiently for cooling in the summer. But while it's still cold outside, it's important to reduce the evaporation of that sweat as much as possible. One way to do that, if you're running, for example, is to map out your route so that you're facing the wind at the beginning and have the wind at your back on the way home. That way, toward the end of your run when you're most sweaty, your course will take you with the wind instead of against, reducing the chill from evaporation.

What you eat and drink before and during cold weather exercise can help prevent minor discomforts as well as major dangers such as hypothermia. First the good news: Food is fuel, so you need to take in more calories during cold weather. Carbohydrates such as natural fruits are always preferable to simple sugars such as candy. And carbohydrates are more readily usable than proteins. Now the bad news: Liquor does not warm you up—it just seems to. So wait until you're indoors and warm. Drinking alcoholic beverages outdoors in cold weather can dull your senses so much that you fail to recognize the warning signs of cold weather hazards.

Cold Weather Hazards

You're not likely to experience any of the real dangers of exposure to extremely cold temperatures when you're jogging around the block in the snow or even playing soccer on the coldest day of the year. But if you plan to go cross-country skiing, or even rock climbing, canoeing or for a trek in the desert in the middle of the summer, you should know the warning signs of hypothermia and frostbite.

If a part of the body is suffering from frostbite, it will look white and feel hard and rigid, painful at first, and then numb. Frostbite, the destruction of body tissue by freezing, occurs when the temperature of the skin drops below 32 degrees, causing the blood vessels to freeze, resulting in no blood circulation in the affected area. You can prevent frostbite by wearing the proper clothing and by making sure the ears, hands and feet are covered. Frostbite responds to rapid treatment: Thaw the area in warm water at 100–108°F., but, according to doctors, do not let the water temperature exceed 112°F.

Hypothermia occurs when the body temperature drops dangerously below its normal 98.6°F. If this internal or core temperature is allowed to drop as much as 14 degrees, you'll lose consciousness; 23 degrees below normal, and death results from heart failure. Although you can't see the body's core temperature, there are plenty of signs warning of hypothermia: slurred speech, a loss of coordination in the hands and feet, a redness of the skin without warming cause, shivering and confusion. At the sign of these symptoms, quickly raise the internal temperature of the body with blankets, other people's warm bodies or a warm bath.

Hot Weather Training

In hot weather the body relies upon evaporation to dissipate its heat and to cool you off. Since you've got to sweat more in the heat, you do sweat more; so you must drink more fluids in the summer for cooling, just as you may need to eat more calories during the winter for heating. You lose water through sweat and through vapor as you breathe out of your mouth and nostrils. An athlete involved in nonstop exercise in the heat can lose four pounds of water in an hour.

Wear clothing that will protect you against the sun and allow perspiration to evaporate. The sun can burn your skin and make you tired if it beats on your head directly. Wear white or light-colored clothing—it reflects the sun's rays, whereas dark colors absorb them and make you hotter. Wear a hat and pour water over it if you want some extra cooling from evaporation. Wear porous materials that allow the air to get to your skin to cool you. All kinds of great fabrics that "breathe" are available at running stores these days.

The best way to avoid the hazards of hot weather exercise (heatstroke and heat exhaustion) is to get into the habit of drinking fluids throughout the day and evening. Water and fruit juices are best because they replenish minerals lost through exercise and because they don't tax the liver to filter out such things as caffeine from coffee and sugar from soda pop. You can drink before, during and after exercise and competition. You can drink up to two cups of fluid every fifteen minutes during exercise without having to sacrifice time to run to the bathroom and without risking stomach cramps or a stitch in your side. Exercise makes the body temporarily cease producing urine, opting to send blood to the working muscles and to the sweating skin rather than to the kidneys. The more you get used to taking in increased amounts of water during the day, the less prone you will become to a stitch in the side or stomach cramps. Such a stitch or cramp is merely the discomfort of too little oxygen reaching the diaphragm. More than two cups of water at a time may distend the stomach so much that it presses on the diaphragm restricting its blood/oxygen supply and making it somewhat painful for you to breathe. But a stitch is easy to get rid of even while you're running if you know a few tricks (see page 163).

On the long swims, when I desperately need fluids and calories to continue, I used to be afraid to drink any quantity of liquids—afraid I would have to quit the race because of cramps or nausea. I quickly learned that the body's collapse from lack of liquids was a far more serious consequence than a stitch in the side. I also learned that practice can help you learn to take in liquids when needed with no negative after-effects whatsoever. I know countless inexperienced marathon runners who reach heat exhaustion and have to quit because they are afraid to take in liquids early on in the race. Make yourself drink in extreme heat—even before you're actually thirsty.

Salt tablets do *not* help you in the heat; in fact they can do much damage. If you need to take in more salt to replenish what is lost through sweat, depend upon your taste buds to tell you by a craving for salty foods.

The heart must work harder to exercise in the heat than in the cold because, in addition to pumping blood to the moving muscles, it must pump more blood to the surface of the skin for sweat. Adapting to hot weather exercise takes about two weeks, but you'll acclimatize faster if you've kept sweating throughout the winter months and if you've kept up your fluid intake all year long. Sweat glands draw fluid from the blood to produce sweat and then transport it to the surface of the skin through the pores. The average female has a fewer number of sweat glands than the average male; therefore, you may sweat less than the men you know. However, this does not mean you have a lower tolerance for the heat. Scientists theorize that, although the female sweats less, she may sweat better. Women may have a more efficient cooling system than men. Though physiologists don't know exactly how this special female cooling mechanism works, they believe it exists since it has been proven that the female adapts to hot weather at least as well and often better than the male without as much fluid loss through sweat.

In any case, high humidity combined with high temperatures is tough on all of us. Since sweat evaporates more slowly under these conditions, the body must compensate by sweating over a greater area of the skin surface. Because it has a greater area to cover, the heart must work harder to pump blood. This is why hot weather exercise requires more fitness and more fluids. One hundred-degree dry heat or 90-degree heat with heavy humidity can drain endurance so that a long-distance runner may take ten to twenty minutes longer to complete a marathon. Or it can drain strength so that a tennis player who usually aces a serve at 100 miles per hour can at best get an 85-mile-per-hour serve across. I spent a few months in Africa. My 12-mile run there took me eighty-two to eighty-five minutes, whereas seventy-two minutes was my norm without the heat. Don't be surprised if you have little energy and your times worsen during high summer. Take all the precautions—lots of fluids, ventilated clothing—and stick with it. Just as training at high altitudes makes you feel great when you get back to the heavy oxygen at sea level, training in extreme heat will be hard work for your heart. But you'll fly come autumn.

Hot Weather Hazards

Some doctors suggest postponing your workout or sports participation if the temperature outdoors is upward of 90°F. combined with 90 percent humidity and no wind velocity. (This advice may ace out Floridians.) Just remember, if your conditioning is fairly good, and if you've been drinking plenty of fluids over a reasonable period of time, you are outfitted to derive safely a good workout and good fun out of almost any day of the year. Be aware, though, of the signals warning of hot weather hazards.

Hypothermia (see page 164) is as much of a hazard in the summer when you'd least expect it to be, as in the winter. Always keep some clothing dry, for the night-time drop in temperature or for when you're wet, tired and a wind comes up. Wet clothing is almost worse than no clothing at all when the body's core temperature has begun to drop because it can make you colder by evaporation and by taking away heat from your skin.

Heat Exhaustion

Heat exhaustion is extreme dehydration, the result of too little fluid intake combined with too much loss of fluid through exercise. Since heat exhaustion takes several days to develop, there is plenty of time to remedy the malaise by taking in more liquids, especially fruit juices. The symptoms are weakness, tiredness, light-headedness—"the mineral blues."

Heatstroke

Heatstroke, due to a sudden rise in body temperature, is dangerous and must be controlled immediately. To prevent it, drink lots of fluids and make sure that you have given yourself several weeks to adapt to the heat before you tax your body with an especially strenuous race or training session in hot weather. Heatstroke is more common in the early spring before joggers have had time to acclimatize themselves to the change in the weather; and it is more prevalent on those days that combine high temperature and high humidity. Heed the warning signs: burning muscles and lungs, labored breathing, dizziness and nausea, blurred vision, irrational behavior.

Treatment for heatstroke must be quick since the syndrome is directly affecting brain cells. Call a doctor right away. Then follow this advice: "If the face is pale, raise the tail; if the face is red, raise the head."

- Lower the victim's temperature by pouring any kind of liquid all over the body to promote cooling by evaporation.

- Rub ice (or very cold water) over the skin to stimulate cooling.

- When the victim regains consciousness into an alert, painless state, stop the treatment; cooling her after she's awake risks the lowering of her body temperature too sharply for safety.

- Maintain a vigil by her side for an hour and if she complains of headache, nausea or dizziness, or if she loses consciousness within that hour, start the treatment all over again.

- As soon as she is alert and without pain, the recovered victim should drink fruit juices because they are rich in the potassium, which can restore the cells to normal.

After recovery, a victim of heatstroke may be more susceptible to the condition for a period of one month if she exercises vigorously. After one month, she will be no more susceptible to heatstroke than anybody else.

You Need Fluids

Drink plenty of fluids, preferably water and fruit juices. You need them for hot weather especially, but as an exerciser you need plenty all year round. Water, as the main component of cells, urine, sweat and blood, is necessary for all the chemical reactions that transport nutrients in and flush waste products out to take place. Nonexercisers need at least six eight-ounce glasses of fluid a day, but since you're in Basic Training, you need more—at least eight glasses daily. Just to show you the extreme, a healthy human can handle up to eighty glasses a day. I drink at least a gallon (sixteen eight-ounce glasses) of water and juices a day. So drink as much as you can.

Drink one or two cups ten minutes before exercise, then one cup at fifteen-minute intervals during, if possible. You can lose between two and four pounds of fluid before you feel thirsty, so anticipate your need and get into the habit of drinking fluids even when you're not thirsty. Drink fruit juices in place of water when you're extra thirsty to avoid that sudden headachy feeling that happens sometimes. It's called water intoxication—brief and harmless but interesting. Water intoxication happens when the abundance of water, which has no minerals, upsets the concentration of minerals inside and outside the cells. Usually the inside and outside concentration is the same, but all this water decreases the concentration of minerals outside the cells, causing fluid to move into the cells to begin to balance that mineral concentration again. When fluid moves into the brain cells, they swell and you feel headachy momentarily, until the concentration of minerals inside and outside the cells returns to normal. The best way to avoid this if you are really thirsty at the moment and want to drink more than two glasses of fluid is to drink fruit juices (or any of the mineral replacement drinks like ERG or Gatorade), which are high in minerals, instead of water.

Of course, all this discussion of fluid loss will mean nothing to you if you don't fully understand the intensity of Basic Training. If you just waltz through your aerobics, this much fluid intake will just bloat you. If you achieve the intensity demanded, this fluid intake will make sense to you.

Miscellanea

Eating before Exercise

If you want to eat a pregame meal for added energy before a big competition or before an especially strenuous workout, be sure to allow at least three hours for digestion. A full stomach depletes the blood supply to the muscles, since the heart is pumping blood to the stomach to digest food. During intense competition, the heart pumps blood to the muscles that need it to contract in vigorous movement. This diminishes the oxygen supply to the stomach and, like any muscle without enough oxygen, the stomach can develop cramps.

The more fit you are and the less intense the exercise, the more food you'll be able to accommodate in your stomach during your workouts. When you are fit, you can handle eating something less than three hours before a workout because your heart is strong enough to pump blood simultaneously to the stomach and to the exercising muscles.

A precompetition meal, taken at least three hours before, should be high in carbohydrates, low in sugar, protein and fat, and it should include at least three glasses of fluid. A good meal like this should further your competitive efforts in three ways: (1) It will be easily digestible; (2) you won't be hungry during competition or your workout; and (3) you'll derive a psychological lift in knowing that you have given your body the best fuel for what it wants to do.

Though this meal is high in carbohydrates, it does not constitute what is known as carbohydrate loading. The idea of carbohydrate loading is that the body will not be clogged up with proteins and fats but will have a high carbohydrate level from which to produce energy two or three days before a major strenuous event such as a marathon. This theory bogs down, in my opinion, because an excess of not-immediately usable carbohydrates is stored as fat anyway. It would make more sense to load carbohydrates the day of the event, when you can really use it.

Age

I don't know where old age falls in a lifetime. There are old thirty-year-olds and young seventy-year-olds. My mother is fifty-five, without a wrinkle on her face, strong as an ox. I have a friend named Sylvia, who lives on a ranch in Baja California, Mexico, who will be seventy-one by the time this book is published. She puts in a full ten hours of hard physical labor every day, yet she has enough energy left at night to make me say "uncle" when we wrestle. And I have a thirty-five-year-old friend who is always complaining of aches, who appears to be perfectly healthy but reclines or sits all day. She becomes exhausted after such strenuous exercise as eating lunch or reading the morning paper. Attitude, obviously, makes you or breaks you.

In fact, older can mean better. Some athletes don't reach their physical peaks until the mid- or late forties: It was only when she was well into her forties that marathon runner Miki Gorman achieved champion status as an American record holder.

The body of a woman in her forties can be better—firmer, leaner, stronger and more attractive—than the body she had in her teens. This is not wishful thinking, this is possible through daily exercise, and we're beginning to hear testimony of it from celebrities in their forties such as Cloris Leachman and Shirley MacLaine. Women I know from ages thirty to fifty tell me that since they began Basic Training, their bodies look and feel better than they ever have in their lives.

If the first forty-five or so years of your life can be spent building to your physical endurance prime, you will surely decline from that peak after age fifty. But if it takes you that long to develop your full physiological potential, then it can also take a long time before you experience a significant loss of it. There is no fountain of youth, but you can restore some of your youthful vigor and slow down the aging process somewhat through regular exercise. The National Institute on Aging states that you can reduce the physiological aging process by 20 percent through exercise. To me that means that the Basic Training athlete will begin to show the normal signs of aging 20 percent later than someone who does not include Basic Training in her lifestyle. Of course, individual and genetic factors can skew an average prediction, but generally I would say that most women with a lifelong commitment to Basic Training could find that at age forty-five they will look thirty and at age sixty they will look forty-five. Most important, you will *feel* youthful and energetic for more of your life with regular exercise.

Advancing age does bring on certain physiological changes that accentuate the need for and the benefits from regular exercise and proper diet. Our metabolism slows as we get older, so we must eat less. Our bones become more brittle, so we become stiffer and more prone to injury. Our skin becomes drier. Energy level slacks off. We (even the Fausts among us) cannot prevent aging; but we can certainly slow it down and make it more comfortable.

I have always thought one of the most criminal myths was that old people should not exercise for fear of stroke or heart attack. Just the contrary! As emphasized throughout Basic Training, regular exercise is the way to prevent stroke and heart attack. Basic Training will unclog your arteries, prevent osteoporosis (brittle bones) and give you more energy. While alleviating constipation, it will allow you to eat more, will relieve insomnia and will make you more limber. Unless you have specific medical instruction to do otherwise, you can start in on Basic Training regardless of your age. It is meant for all women—for life. I plan to be out there doing my aerobics, weights, 90/90's and stretching on my last day.

I find most older people like to swim for the Basic Training aerobics, because swimming is so kind to the joints, but if you are a runner, cyclist or rope skipper, very high temperatures and very high humidity make the heart work much harder than usual. If you feel at all faint or light-headed or nauseated on these days, skip it. Wait for a break in the weather, then get back out there.

You may feel embarrassed that your legs don't look tight and smooth as they did thirty years ago or that you really feel out of place among the twenty-year-old body-beautifuls at the weight room. Don't be embarrassed; you are not unique in your aging. But you *will* be unique in pursuing muscle tone and fitness for your current potential.

I have always been pleased by the respect given the older women by the younger in my weight room. They deserve it.

Pregnancy

Unless a special medical problem dictates otherwise, you can continue Basic Training during pregnancy and derive double benefit. I hope there are no old-school obstetricians left who are advocating nine months of little to no movement—much less active exercise—and a huge weight gain. Theories have changed: In most cases, pregnant women should be quite active and should keep their weight gain under control. The more muscle tone and fitness the mother has, the easier the birth, both for her and the baby. Basic Training, don't forget, is the absolute minimum a woman should do for her body. It is not an extreme routine that produces exhaustion, undue stress on the heart or potential damage to the bones or organs.

During pregnancy, swimming is the optimal choice among the six aerobic activities. Not only might skipping rope or running be difficult but the jarring might be hazardous in the last few months. I know many women who swim vigorously right up to the last day—flip turns and everything! Second, although the stretching and the aerobics are advisable throughout pregnancy, lifting weights—especially at the intensity level required in Basic Training—is an individual option. Consult your doctor. Of course, you want to maintain muscle tone, and muscle strength helps in childbirth itself, but your doctor may suggest less strenuous ways of doing this. I have had pregnant friends who have lifted right up to the last day, but these were women who had been lifting weights for years—the fundamentals of Basic Training were not new to them.

One other item for those of you who are or plan to become pregnant. Often, pregnancy is the first time in a woman's life when she really attempts to learn something about nutrition and sticks to what she learns—for the baby's sake. Again, your doctor will give you the bottom line on what's in and what's out, and you will no doubt be reading a host of thorough literature on nutrition. I have outlined some of the neglected basics in the Diet Primer. Just like the Basic Training exercises, if it applies to nonpregnant women, it applies to you twofold. Who knows—you may be one of the wise individuals who continues to eat well after your baby is born.

Menstruation

There are no drugs, no foods, no drinks, no breathing or meditation exercises, no mantras that can alleviate menstrual cramps and discomfort as regular, strenuous exercise can. I have never had a menstrual cramp or a moment's menstrual discomfort in my life. I have recommended Basic Training to women who do have some degree of menstrual discomfort; 100 percent of these women have reported back that their problem has either disappeared completely or eased considerably.

A small percentage of women experience real agony with their periods; they run a fever, are doubled over and must go to bed for 24 to 48 hours until the pain subsides. This is not psychosomatic, as some doctors diagnose it; it is an actual physiological problem, often resulting from the constriction of capillaries and other blood vessels throughout the reproductive organs. Even in these extreme cases, regular participation in Basic Training has reduced the pain to a tolerable level for most without medication or strict bed rest; and a few (my head trainer is one) have delighted in the complete disappearance of monthly agony.

Regular is the key word in any case where exercise alleviates menstrual cramps. Waiting for the day your period starts won't help. It is exercise as a life-style, not a now-and-then remedy for what ails you, that improves circulation, unclogs the blood vessels and strengthens the abdominal muscles—

all factors conducive to painless menstruation. Keep in mind also that dozens of world records have been set by women during menstruation. Likewise, as a Basic Training athlete, you need not feel any worse—tired or slow or stiff—during menstruation; and if you do, start and finish your workout anyway. There will never be any danger in doing so, only benefit.

Irregular or even nonexistent periods are possible during your first year of Basic Training. A very rare occurrence for anyone who is not in *extreme* training, the cessation of your periods should be discussed with a gynecologist. In most cases, she can reassure you that it is a sign of health during heavy exercise, and nothing to worry about. If your menstrual cycle changes, it is probably because your fat percentage is dropping to the point that the body knows it is not fat enough to support a pregnancy, so it doesn't ovulate for the time being.

Depression

You needn't be at the brink of hospitalization to have experienced depression. We all have felt a few hours, a few days or even a few weeks of dejected spirit and dulled vitality. We have all been brought to a point of immobility over a death, a slap to the ego over loss of a job or a lover, an approaching thirtieth birthday or simply some chemical reaction of unknown description within us. In every case, the best antidote for depression is movement.

Women who have opted for exercise instead of pill popping to exorcise their personal demons are far better off for it. Exercise as well as regular sport participation can become a positive addiction, as natural to humans as play, and it can replace a negative dependence on drugs, alcohol or food. Just as no one has really pinpointed why play is fun, so too scientists have so far been unable to discover exactly why physical exercise improves mood and increases one's sense of well-being. Perhaps an increase in blood supply to the brain, a fostering of sound and deeper sleep through physical exercise, or merely the psychological satisfaction of accomplishing a difficult task or performing beyond your expectations helps. One theory suggests that exercise increases the level of a hormone called *norepinephrine* in the bloodstream. People who feel happy have been found to have high levels of norepinephrine in the bloodstream, whereas people who suffer depression have low levels.

So if you're down about something specific or just down in general, if you can't seem to summon the energy to get out of your chair (from depression, not exhaustion), make sure of two things. One, eliminate sugar from your diet. Sugar, as well as alcohol and barbiturates, is among the worst depressants we know of (see Diet Primer). And second, get off your duff, get moving and do your Basic Training exercises for the day. Your coach guarantees that you'll feel better.

How to Cheat on Basic Training

I have a trainer on my long swims who wants me to make it to the other shore as much as I do. She knows exactly what it's going to take of me and she helps me design my swim training program with meticulous care. And then she is with me every day of that intense training season, making sure I stick to that program. We both know that I am not going to make it on the big day if I fool around during preparation. However, occasionally, let's say two or three times a swim season, I become thoroughly depleted—either physically or mentally or both—and she knows it. About six weeks before my 89-mile swim in 1979, Margie was following in a boat alongside me as usual when she realized something—something only a trainer can observe or know by instinct. She recognized that to push me farther would tear either my body or my spirit down beyond the point of easy recuperation.

So, during the third hour of that eight-hour training swim in the ocean, to my great surprise, she stopped the boat, blew the whistle, signaled me over and dragged me over the gunwales. As I lay happily on the floorboards, she sang, told jokes and, while heading full throttle back to shore, said, "You're going to have a long, hot bath, a massage and then we're going to the movies!" I was ecstatic. In the tub, on the massage table, watching the movie, I had the delicious feeling that I was cheating, that I successfully skipped out on some drudgery I was supposed to be doing.

I hope that Basic Training will never seem like drudgery to you. I know you will never reach the point of physical or spiritual depletion—it's not demanding enough for that. Nevertheless, there will be days when cheating—skipping what you're supposed to do—will be just the ruse you need to renew your enthusiasm. As we all know, the thrill of cheating is in not getting caught. You'll get caught—you'll feel and show a lack of fitness and muscle tone—if you cheat more often than you play fair with yourself. The trick to successful cheating, then, is to be a Basic Training stickler as a general rule. Cheating will never become that delicious thrill unless you have really made Basic Training a steady, daily, uncompromising routine. The more dedicated to Basic Training you become, the better able will you be to distinguish between the days when you *need* to give yourself a swift kick in the behind to get out there and the days when you *need* to go to the movies. You'll know—the delight comes only when you *need* the break.

If you want to cheat on Basic Training *without* getting caught, do the following substitute program on your "cheating" days:

1. Skip rope 300 times; 100 skips at a time with a 30-second rest in between. Then, in any order:
2. Do 30 push-ups, however you can get them; 10 at a time with rest in between, if you like.
3. Do 100 side-bends (see page 125), 50 on each side.
4. Do 15a (leg raises in Weight-Training Manual) for 60 continuous seconds.
5. Do 13a (abductor kicks in Weight-Training Manual), first 20 on the right leg, then 20 on the left leg.
6. Do one 90/90 instead of both (see page 78).
7. Do 11a (donkey kicks; 11a in Weight-Training Manual) 20 times with each leg.

CHAPTER 10

The Sport and Health Club Primer

If you've ever had fun, then you already know the most important thing to know about sport. Sport is whatever you enjoy doing. And some people enjoy games and competition. You may be someone who would thrive on competition and doesn't know it because your first early introduction to sports competition was problematic, unpleasant or even non-existent. Well, there's still time. Women pros in tennis are close to achieving parity in prize money with men, federal law (Title IX) mandates equal opportunity for females in school athletics and social restrictions have eased up, freeing the woman of average athletic talent to participate and not just look on.

I am not personally welcomed with ticker-tape parades or $100,000 checks when I crawl out on the opposite shore after finishing a swim. But I have received thousands of letters, mostly from women and girls. On my thirtieth birthday, the day after I completed the longest swim in history (89 miles from the Bahamas to Florida), one of the birthday cards I received was from a class of twelve-year-old girls, each telling me what she wanted to become. Carefully wrapped in tissue paper, the card's art-work read, "Happy Birthday, Earth's Greatest Swimmer." Males may have been the first to set a dusty foot on the moon, but to those twelve-year-old girls, the greatest swimmer in the earth's oceans is a woman.

This is progress. There were women sports her-oes yesterday, there are more today and there will be more recognized tomorrow. And as far as participation for fun and competition goes, sports are wide open for girls and women now. You can take your pick.

Sports were not methodically designed to make you as fit as possible. Of course, in some sports (especially the aerobic sports but also basketball, soccer, downhill skiing, racquetball and others) you can achieve a high development of muscle tone, strength, cardiovascular efficiency and flexibility as side effects when you play or participate regularly. But Basic Training is designed specifically for total fitness and you may *not* substitute sports for your Basic Training workouts. Sports offer other benefits, all extremely valuable. To play almost any sport well, you must call into play concentration, imagination, versatility, confidence, control of your emotions, calmness under pressure and the ability to share glory, win graciously or accept defeat.

But first, always, sports are fun. The process is a joyous circle: The more fun you have, the more you play or participate; the more you participate, the better you become; the better you become, the more fun you have. Professional and elite athletes have no monopoly on sports enjoyment; in fact, it may be easier for those of you who participate in sports as an avocation instead of a job to experience the pure thrill of competition—your contract or your future is never on the line. The occasional moment of perfection, as in a diving catch or a smoothly executed passing shot, is available to everybody who goes at her sport with a 100 percent effort. Something of the feline perfection of movement—quickness and directness, no motion wasted—can be available to you, too.

What you play is up to you. There are as many different kinds of sports and activities as there are different personalities and types of athletic skills. If you have good eye–hand coordination, for instance, a racquet sport might be best for you. If you're quick on your feet, try basketball or soccer. If you're independent, possessed of good imagination and enjoy competing against yourself, get into an individual sport like swimming or long-distance running. If you're short on self-discipline and long on sociability, try a team sport like soccer or volleyball, full of continuous action on everybody's part.

When choosing a sport, think about whether you're better suited to individual or to team activity. The former is probably more accessible to you, unless you're still in school. Individual sports require little organization. Often you need only a single other player or no partner at all; you need not recruit nine others as you would for a basketball game. Individual sports can teach you a lot about yourself. Looking an opponent in the eye across a tennis net, competing in the close quarters of a racquetball court, accepting your own victory or defeat, does much for emotional maturity. You learn self-reliance.

Some, though, find individual sport too solitary. These people pursue their competitive selves in team activities. Team sport still requires you to perform under pressure, perhaps even more so since there are others depending on you. It teaches you how to get along with others—teamwork, cooperation, communication—you don't always shoot if it's better to pass. You support your teammates and they encourage you in return. Team sport helps to build friendships; getting your shins kicked as a group does wonders in forming lasting bonds.

Basic Training cannot be replaced by sports activity, but if you participate in a sport *in conjunction* with Basic Training, your athletic ability will be greatly enhanced. Basic Training will make your body strong, fit and flexible so that your chances of

injury while playing a sport will be minimized and your performance will improve markedly. I call my co-author Candace Lyle Hogan a natural athlete. Candace is blessed with natural strength, coordination and quickness, but she never had the opportunity to develop these athletic gifts with regular coaching. She used to be the best soccer, softball, table-tennis player among her peer group without practicing. Then she committed herself to Basic Training. Basic Training dramatically improved an already good athlete. At age thirty-three she can now run like the wind throughout a 90-minute soccer game without pacing herself; she can now hit homers regularly *and* play first base in softball; and she can retrieve topspin slams in table tennis with consistent quickness and accuracy.

Basic Training will strengthen your quadriceps and help you to jump higher in basketball and volleyball; it will strengthen your wrist to allow you to hit faster-paced shots in racquetball and squash and to achieve better distance in golf; it will give all your leg muscles strength and endurance for skiing, soccer, cycling, field hockey and dance; your upper body will be strong and flexible for gymnastics, motocross, swimming, rowing and all racquet sports. You will tire much less easily; you will be quicker; you will be more intense and accurate. The regular, precise discipline of Basic Training will become a good habit to carry over into your sport.

Health Clubs

You don't need to join a health or fitness club to do Basic Training. You can buy a set of free weights or devise them at home for strength building; and you can simply run or bicycle outdoors for aerobics. However, sometimes for less than what it costs to go to a movie once a week, you can purchase a yearly membership to a club. Access to a fitness club offers many advantages. First and foremost, having a particular place to go where you can take care of every phase of your workouts can help you fit Basic Training into your life regularly, and when you are paying money for facilities, you are more likely to use them on a regular schedule. Second, clubs provide you with "perks." You can reward yourself after a tough workout with a whirlpool bath, a sauna, a dip in the pool or even a couple of games of racquetball or table tennis if you have time. And third, a club is a good place for camaraderie with other people who share your interest in fitness; and if you join with a friend, you can help each other, physically and psychologically, with your Basic Training workouts.

Health clubs have become so popular that there is a type available now to fit almost any personality. Across the country, health and fitness clubs fall into several basic categories with different emphases:

- spas for women concentrating on weight loss and figure improvement;
- low-key coed clubs offering (in the pool, sauna, whirlpool) a more subtle socializing alternative to singles bars and discos;
- serious coed fitness clubs with trainers to coach strength building and cardiovascular conditioning;
- clubs from the inexpensive Y to the elite racquet sport clubs where fitness becomes secondary to sport competition or dance and yoga classes.

Of course, I'm partial to the third type, but as long as a club affords you the facilities you need and full access to them, it will do fine. Be wary of scams, however. This industry has mushroomed in the past few years, carrying a lot of fly-by-night operators with it. And remember, it's not important that women have pastel-blue equipment and that men have black Naugahyde upholstery: In fact, the prettier it is, the more you're probably paying for it. Men and women can use the same machinery; all you need to do sometimes is adjust the seat-height or add a cushion if you're not tall enough to achieve the perfect position. Be wary of hidden costs and downright fraud.

You already know that the main thing to consider before selecting a club is what your aims are and how much time it will take to achieve those goals daily and weekly. You know that your aim is to perform Basic Training regularly and that takes an average of 30 minutes a day (or 1 hour on weight-training days). Decide what time of day you'll need to use a club for your Basic Training according to your weekly schedule. Then find out how busy the club is during those hours. You may want to double-check the manager's answer to that question by visiting the club during the hour of the day you plan to use it, and by asking a member at random how busy the club usually gets. If you're going to have to wait around for Nautilus machines or stationary bicycles to be available for your use during certain hours, either rearrange your schedule to go during off-hours if you can, or else find another club that has more room and facilities. (You should be able to go from machine to machine without waiting more than a minute so that you don't get stiff by cooling off and let your pulse drop and so that you don't waste time.)

If the yearly membership fee is steep, you should be getting a wide range of most of the following facilities: Nautilus, Universal, free weights, treadmills, stationary bikes, swimming pool, sauna, whirlpool, steam room, some floor space to do your stretching exercises and, of course, a women's locker room with showers and hair dryers provided for your use by the management. Some clubs even offer free yoga, dance, martial arts or calisthenics classes hourly in addition to trainers who are ready to help you and answer your questions. Some clubs house a food or juice bar as well as a locker-room attendant with an array of shampoos, creams, bathing suits and caps, locks and towels for rent or sale. Decide what you need and what you're willing to pay for beforehand, and then go shopping for a club armed with that information.

When you approach club representatives, be sure to ask them enough questions to assure yourself that you'll be getting what you're paying for. Then make sure that what they're saying is available is actually written into the contract. Never sign anything without knowing exactly what you're obligating yourself for, and never sign a contract without reading it carefully. Some states have passed specific laws to protect the consumer from health club fraud. Make sure that the price of membership gives you access to all the club facilities you want at all the hours and on all the days you'll be needing them. Contracts ought to give you a cancellation clause if you move outside the area (20 miles away from the club), if you die or if under doctor's orders you can't receive the services. Also there should be a money-back cancellation clause if there is good reason to be dissatisfied with the quality or availability of facilities promised. Because you are a club member, your renewal fee the next year should be less than the rate for the beginning member. Some clubs offer special rates if you join with a friend or family member as well as special discounts on your renewal fee should you be responsible for bringing in a friend who decides to join.

You should also find out some information that you may not get from directly questioning the management: How safe from crime are the inner and outer environs of the club for a woman? What is the attitude of club trainers toward women? Ask current members these questions. Make sure the streets are well lit in the area in and outside the club; that

there is well-lighted, inexpensive parking nearby and/or a bike rack outside the club if you plan to use the two-wheel mode of transportation.

Health and Safety Rules

The Locker Room
- Bring your own lock and towel—it's cheaper than renting each time. Buy a combination lock so that you don't have to carry a key with you into the weight room. (If you use a lock with a key, attach the key to a wide rubber band and wear it around your wrist.)
- *Never* leave your belongings unattended, even for a minute.
- Don't forget to lock your locker. (Some clubs will rent you your own permanent locker for a monthly fee so you don't have to carry your bathing suit and workout clothes back and forth every day.)

Your Personal Approach to the Locker Room

I am so accustomed to training around men that I had to be reminded that many women feel very uncomfortable doing so, at least for the first few times. Nowadays girls and boys take physical education classes together, but when we over-thirty-year-olds grew up, high school gym classes were sex-separate. So you might feel self-conscious entering the weight-training room initially, either because it is filled predominantly with men or because you're appearing in "public" in clothes that reveal your body, or because of some combination of the two. Here are some tips to use to fortify yourself for that first entry into the weight room or exercise class at a health club. But first recognize what a health club is and what a health club is not.

Let's dispel right away any lingering notion that a health club is like a singles bar. Anyone who might be trying to use it as a way to meet a prospective date is not getting his workout done properly and so is wasting his membership fee. Although it's possible to meet new people, this is a secondary benefit. Working out with the proper intensity and precision takes so much concentration that even when a person has the roving eye he is not able to use it in the weight room. People go to a health club to work intensely on their own, and they respect other people who are there to do likewise. People in a weight room appreciate an atmosphere of hard work and concentration. But, anyway, you're not there to impress anybody or to worry about what any-

one might be thinking. You're there for yourself, so here's how to approach it:

- Walk into the weight room as if you belong there. *You do.* If you cower in the corner, you'll be licked by your self-consciousness before you even start. No self-deprecating giggles please; you should act as if you owned the place. Remember that people are involved in their own workouts. If they notice you at all, they'll only recognize that you're working hard and will respect you for it.
- Keep in mind that yours will be neither the best body in the room nor the worst. Remember that everyone al-

The Weight Room

- Wear rubber-soled shoes in the weight room—a place with heavy weights and machinery is no place to go barefoot.
- Wear cotton socks to absorb sweat and prevent blisters. Take along a small towel to dry off the seats.
- Wear shorts or sweat pants when using the weight room facilities.
- Obey the rules of the weight room: Always put the weights back where you found them on the rack (they're usually arranged in order, light to heavy); fold over the Velcro straps on the Nautlius machines to protect them from the carpet fuzz.
- Never bang the plates on Nautilus and Universal machines; let them down lightly when you're through with an exercise. This is just common sense, and it keeps the equipment from wearing out too fast (and might even keep the club from raising its rates too rapidly to accommodate equipment replacement)!
- You can drink water between exercises, as long as it's not more than a cup every 10 minutes or so.

The Spa Area

- Get yourself a pair of rubber flip-flops or something easy to slip on your feet in the showers, sauna and pool areas. Even when a club is kept very clean, there is still the danger of athlete's foot with so many people using the facilities.
- Avoid tanning rooms. Ultraviolet light can be hazardous to the skin and to the eyes. If you use them, don't stay under them longer than one minute, and keep your eyes shut. *My advice is not to use them at all.*
- If you use the pool, get used to a pair of plastic goggles. Not only do they provide comfort and ease in swimming, but they help prevent infection in the tear-duct glands.

---

ways wishes she had someone else's body—so just as you are thinking, "I wish I had her thin legs," she is thinking about you, "I wish I had her flat tummy."

- You're not in competition with the men or the other women. Women tend to feel an immediate camaraderie, not competitiveness, with other women in a weight room; and men tend to feel either oblivious of the presence of women there or else respectful of the ones who are working hard. Just as a 200-pound man can respect a 150-pound man who has assertiveness and intensity but lesser size or absolute strength, he can also respect a woman who has that assertiveness and intensity.

- Don't care what anyone thinks: You're not there to apply for a job or to get a date.
- Remember your advantage over other people in the weight room: You have a specific plan. You're not there just to do a few sit-ups and jumping jacks—you are doing Basic Training, a set regimen. After walking in, get to work on it: Find the first machine you need; look for the next station after that, and so on, step by step. Concentrate on Basic Training; be purposeful; you know what you're doing.
- And, finally, a subjective opinion. Take it from me, women who aren't used to exercising in public always come out in leotards. The image of the leotard does not evoke glamour in the weight room but rather the assumption that the person wearing it has no idea what she's doing there. Unless you are a dancer, don't wear a leotard. It's hard to sweat in one—it closes off the pores. The same thing holds true for nylon stockings—they're unnecessary and constricting. Today the much more appropriate weight room dress, allowing for freer movement and skin-breathing, is a loose pair of shorts, a cotton T-shirt, socks and sneakers. I like running shorts that weigh no more than two ounces, have an elastic stretch band at the waist and can be washed and dried by machine.

- If you play racquet sports like squash or racquetball at your club, *always* wear protective eyeglasses on the court.

- Although clubs use a lot of chlorine for sanitary purposes, *always* be sure to wash your crotch carefully after sitting in whirlpool baths. Use a towel to sit or lie upon in the steam room and the sauna.

- A good pool temperature for lap swimming is between 78 and 80 degrees Fahrenheit.

- The Consumer Product Safety Commission recommends (but does not mandate) that the whirlpool bath in your club be kept at 104 degrees Fahrenheit; but at my club, members complained that it wasn't hot enough, so it was raised to 106 degrees.

- Don't stay in the sauna, steam room or whirlpool bath for more than 10 minutes. Get out immediately if you feel faint or in any way woozy.

- Drink water before and after you get into any of these three hot, soothing facilities because they have a dehydrating effect.

- *Always* take a shower after your Basic Training workout before going outside again. Even though you might feel invigorated, even when you're too tired, do not fail to take a warm shower and to dry your hair. A hot shower might feel good on your muscles, but take an extra minute to turn to a cooler temperature before you dry off. You should not be hot and sweaty when you leave the club; it's important to get your body temperature back to normal. Be dry and warm before you go outdoors again, no matter what time of year it is, but especially in winter.

You Have a Right to Be There

If you haven't entered a gym in twenty years, you might expect to feel funny walking into a roomful of sweating, grunting men working out with weights at a coed club. Just remember, everyone is there for the same general purpose, and as a full-fledged member, you have as much right to be there as anybody else. Don't be intimidated by the men in the weight room; whoever is there is not there to be mean to you or to flirt with you. Despite the relative bareness of the bodies all about, a weight-training room is a rather asexual environment. There may be mirrors galore, but they're not used for vanity so much as for checking out the precision of form during an exercise. People come in all shapes and sizes, and it doesn't matter how attractive you do or don't look in a weight room. I wear shorts and a T-shirt; no special apparel is necessary. The important thing is that you can work out efficiently and comfortably in whatever you're wearing.

As a beginner you're bound to make a few mistakes, but everybody is so busy making her own minor mistakes that she's not going to notice yours. No one is going to laugh at you; and don't laugh at yourself either. Simply be as serious as you need to be in order to concentrate on what you're doing. You're in the weight room to do your Basic Training workout. Save the socializing for the locker room, for the whirlpool bath, for later.

One last note but an important one: Your work place may have fitness and/or sports facilities. Many large corporations have begun to install gymnasiums for their employees as a work incentive, as a productivity booster, as a preventive form of health insurance. Women should have equal access to all such facilities.

CHAPTER 11

The Diet Primer

If we are to believe popular magazines and television talk shows, losing weight is the biggest single preoccupation of American women. If calories are not actually in our mouths, then calories are on our chatting tongues constantly. Being perpetually on a diet is the one thing all women supposedly have in common. But what a negative common link that is! I'm hoping that, if nothing else, the effect of this book will be to substitute in the conversation among women the phrase "Oh, I'm so fat!" with "Say, I'm getting so strong!"

Once you understand how to use Basic Training it should be your answer to weight control. My mother feels she has had a weight problem all her life. Even though she eats a moderate, healthy diet and keeps active throughout the week, she is constantly fighting excess fat. This is not a weight problem. She is suffering from a natural female phenomenon—unlike men, women cannot maintain a lean weight simply by eating well and keeping active. My mother needs to discover that a minimal amount of daily high-intensity calorie-burning Basic Training would inspire her to eat even better and would relieve her endless preoccupation with her weight. The problem is that just as I didn't want to hear my mother's lectures when I was twelve, she doesn't want to hear my lectures now. She will have to discover Basic Training in her own time.

In fact, "losing weight" is an inaccurate way to talk about reducing body-fat percentage. What you lose through exercise combined with proper nutrition is not necessarily weight, but rather fat. Muscle weighs more than fat. So unless you are obese, the muscle tone you gain may outweigh the body

fat you lose; and your progress may never show up on the bathroom scale. However, it will show up in the mirror. Firm muscle makes you look slimmer even though you may weigh the same or even more. Also, the muscle you build in the shoulders will make your hips look more slender and your entire body more proportionate. Unless you are obese, you've got to stop being so concerned with "losing weight" and start being proud of gaining muscle and losing fat through Basic Training.

So how do you reduce your body-fat percentage? Exercise is only half the answer. The rest is diet—not going on a diet necessarily—but adjusting your eating habits so that you don't eat to excess and you don't eat dangerously.

At thirty-two years of age, having always considered myself a healthy specimen, I was shocked to discover how poorly I had been eating all these years. Like most other Americans, I was brought up to believe that steak is the most nutritious food in the world and that a candy bar or some form of sugar is the best energy source when you need a lift. My ignorance, especially when you consider that sport is my vocation and my body is my instrument in sport, was astounding. I am just now beginning to learn what a strain I have been putting on most systems of my body by poor diet.

Nutrition—the study of what the body needs to take in and in what amounts and proportions—is a field in its infancy, especially in this country. (When I was in Japan last year, I was amazed at how lean and healthy everyone looked. Hardly anybody in Japan is fat! The Japanese don't eat red meat, whole milk or refined sugar. Their diet consists primarily of fresh vegetables, fish, and fresh fruit instead of dessert.) I accept two facts: One, it is becoming clear, by almost daily nutritional discoveries, that the typical American diet is one of the leading causes of heart disease today. Two, along with regular strenuous exercise, a dramatic change in that diet is the only hope for widespread good health. This book focuses on the other road to good health—regular, strenuous exercise. I am not a nutrition expert and this is not a diet book; however, I feel it would in some way be wrong of me not to set down the basics of nutrition for you, as I understand them. After all, Basic Training is dedicated to your *overall* health, and exercise is only half the story.

Exercise and nutrition complement each other. In fact, I believe that exercise in the form of Basic Training is the part of the process toward good health that will make the other component—good eating habits—easier for you to attain. Eating wisely takes discipline and a good self-image. The discipline you demonstrate in your daily commitment to Basic Training (and the good self-image you build) should spill over into other areas of your life, notably diet. If you're fat, you practice bad eating habits and suffer a low self-image. It's hard to break out of old patterns. But it's easier to change a habit once you have created a new pattern in some other area. Through Basic Training you will probably be changing a sedentary habit into an active one. Once you do that, you should find breaking out of old eating patterns easier for you psychologically.

My information as to which things you should and should not consume, under "Do's" and "Don'ts" to follow, is just an outline of the basics. I hope that you will become concerned enough about the quality of your diet to seek further information. Check the agricultural extension service of your state university, and write the FDA and the USDA for pamphlets. You may find, as I have, that your eating habits are not as healthy as you thought.

The goal of a good nutritional program is the maintenance of normal weight and blood pressure. It is a myth that your weight should increase as you get older. Your metabolism will probably slow down as you get older, so you will have to eat less to maintain your ideal weight, but you should maintain the same weight throughout your adult life.

There are so many myths and fads associated with reducing diets and sports diets that some basic truths need to be emphasized. (Some world-class athletes swear by milkshakes and Twinkies, whereas others believe in beer and potato chips, or fasting, or steak and potatoes, or natural grains and alfalfa sprouts.) Remember, though, that what follow are merely my *opinions*, gleaned from my own reading and my own life. And, too, in the area of diet as in no other section of this book, I do not always practice to the letter what I preach. I'm trying, though, and you should too.

First the basics, then the do's and don'ts. All the following tips on nutrition revolve around two central truths: (1) Nutrition is a key to preventive medicine, our chance to *create* our own good health rather than desperately seek a cure when illness strikes; (2) good nutrition over a long period can reverse damage done previously by poor nutrition, regardless of your past eating habits. There's hope!

Don'ts

Though I am still sometimes confused as to exactly what I *should* eat, it's really fairly easy to pinpoint—and eliminate—the obvious things that my body *doesn't* need and *can't* use. To maintain my ideal weight, I cannot consume more calories than I can burn. I also know that what kind of food I eat is equally important. For example, if I eat 1,200 calories of carbohydrates (fruits, vegetables and grains) I am likely to burn all of those calories with my intense exercise routine. But if I eat 1,200 calories of fatty food (red meat and dairy products) most of those will be stored as fat. The following list of "don'ts" contains foods that most of us consume regularly and needlessly. We eat them even though they are harmful and often difficult to digest. Most of us are practically addicted to one or more of them, and to eliminate an addiction necessitates an entire change in life-style. It is not easy, and you may not succeed. My downfall is sugar. My habit is so strong, and my addiction so great, that, even knowing what I know now about the evils of sugar, I have not yet given it up completely. I have cut down dramatically, but I know that I must decide soon, for the sake of my future health, to let it go forever. Your downfall might be the caffeine in your morning coffee or the heavy salting of your food. If you actually take some time to pursue the subject of nutrition and read some good literature, you will be convinced not only that you can live without these things but also that your enjoyment of other, healthy foods is enhanced.

Sugar

Glycogen (a usable simple sugar converted from the food you eat) is the source of energy for all movement, but the best sources of glycogen are the complex carbohydrates such as fruits, vegetables and grains. The simple carbohydrates, or simple sugars—candy, honey, ice cream, syrups, jellies, cakes, pies, soft drinks, processed cereals, doughnuts, refined and bleached breads—have almost no food value, only calories. People in the United States, on the average, eat their own weight in useless sugar every year. And sugar is a killer. It contributes to obesity. It raises the levels of both cholesterol and fats in the blood and is thereby implicated in atherosclerosis, heart attack and stroke. Equally serious, the regular intake of excessive sugar can hasten the onset of diabetes, its opposite, hypoglycemia, and wreak havoc in general upon the whole adrenal/insulin hormonal system.

Unlike complex carbohydrates, which cause the blood-sugar level to rise gradually, simple sugars force the blood-sugar level sky high suddenly, as soon as you eat them. This sudden rise in the blood-sugar level sends a red alert to the islets of Langerhans in the pancreas. When the islets of Langerhans receive this emergency message, they manufacture insulin like mad and the insulin then lowers the blood-sugar level too much. The low blood-sugar level makes you feel down, depressed and hungry soon again—craving sugar to raise your blood-sugar level quickly and make you feel up again. It's a vicious, unsatisfying cycle. I know people who eat so much sugar in their daily diet that they wake up in the morning with a crashing hangover—the low from the low blood-sugar level—without having drunk a drop of alcohol the night before. They have a couple of sweet rolls for breakfast to get over that hangover, and the blood-sugar level skyrockets and dips all over again.

If you've got a sweet tooth, eat fruit. Fruit contains fructose, which takes longer to break down than the glucose in simple sugars. Fruit gives you a boost of carbohydrate energy while diminishing the bad effects of "roller coaster sugar" in your bloodstream.

Fats

Fats come under both Do's and Don'ts. You need some fat. But almost half of the calories consumed by a typical American today comes from fats! This gross amount of fats is either stored as excess blubber, which forces the heart and muscles to work much harder when at rest as well as when at work, or, if saturated, raises the fat level in the blood—a proven cause of heart attack and stroke. Many doctors and nutritionists recommend monounsaturated fats, like olive oil, or polyunsaturated fats, like liquid vegetable oils (corn, cottonseed, safflower), instead of fats that come in solid form (saturated fats), like animal fat and butter.

Your best bet is to eat as little fat as possible; no more than 10 percent of your daily caloric intake should be fats. Ten percent is a maximum; some nutritionists urge no more than 1 percent.

Salt

Humans need only one-fifth of a gram of salt per day; however, most Americans take in 18 grams a day. Most of the foods Americans eat are full of salt—it's an invisible ingredient in most processed foods, meat and poultry. The one-fifth of a gram we need daily regulates where and how water is distributed in the body. Excess salt interferes with the body's ability to retain water. People tend to think that because salt is lost in sweat, the body needs to be fortified with salt tablets. However, salt tablets can be extremely dangerous, especially in sports or workouts in hot weather, because they make you vulnerable to heat exhaustion or even heatstroke, which can kill (see Hot Weather Training, page 165).

An even more dangerous result of excess salt intake is high blood pressure or hypertension. In this case, excess salt can be a killer. Try to shoot for no more than one-fifth of a gram per day.

Caffeine

Caffeine comes in jolting doses in coffee, in tea and in soft drinks. It also occurs in smaller amounts in some cocoas and chocolates. Caffeine has been associated with heart palpitations (tachycardia), which can predispose one to heart attack. Though caffeine studies today have only progressed to roughly the same point cigarette studies were fifteen years ago, I myself stay away from caffeine. There are decent decaffeinated coffees and teas available.

Cholesterol

Cholesterol is important for many body functions. It is vital to the production of bile, the insulation of the nerves, and the defense against infection, among other things. But excess cholesterol just collects in the blood and sticks to walls of arteries in the form of plaque, blocking the flow of blood, causing heart attack and stroke. Because cholesterol is found in all animal products but not in vegetables, and because we need the protein and cholesterol of animal products in only minimal amounts, I recommend that you obtain your protein mostly from nonmeat sources (see pages 184 and 185). I feel strongly that you should go to the extra expense of having your cholesterol level checked during your yearly physical examination, as regularly as you check your blood pressure. Look for a good, safe low reading of 145 to 155, 75 points below the national average, 75 points safer from heart disease. If you are in the 200 range, cut back on animal products, especially beef.

Drugs

We used to talk wondrously of "miracle drugs"; now we talk of a national problem called "drug abuse." We pop pills at a perilous rate and at the slightest hint of mental or physical discomfort.

My advice is simple. Be very careful what drugs you take in. Ask the physician or pharmacist exactly what he's giving you and be sure you receive detailed instructions about how much and how often to take a prescribed drug. If you're taking a combination of drugs, double-check that it's a safe combination.

And *never take diet pills*. More than two million people in the United States use amphetamines, stimulants that retard fatigue and supposedly help one lose weight. Called uppers in the vernacular, amphetamines alter one's judgment; and in sports they can make you more susceptible to injury and heatstroke by rendering you oblivious to warning signs of pain or fatigue. As with other drugs, the effectiveness of uppers diminishes with use, necessitating increased dosages to achieve the same psychological effect—the mistaken *belief* that you function better on drugs in your work and in your relationships with other people. Uppers, downers, hallucinogens and narcotics such as heroin, all take you to the same place—nowhere.

Alcohol

Several recent theories suggest that small doses of wine or beer once a day can be healthy. They postulate that small amounts of alcohol aid digestion and that beer replenishes important minerals (like magnesium) lost during exercise. But even if the breweries and vineyards are the ones circulating these theories, the problem seems to be that very few people indulge in alcoholic beverages to a small degree. And *too much* alcohol consumption is addictive. Besides, liquor is so high in sugar content that the blood-sugar level goes low enough to cause depression, or what you may know as a hangover. In order to feel good again, you take another drink to shoot sugar back into the bloodstream. Alcoholism is one of the most widespread, and saddest, diseases in this country.

Tobacco

No one should doubt the surgeon general's findings that cigarette smoking is dangerous to your health. Smoking tobacco—especially the way it is chemically processed in this country—not only leads to illness but also becomes a slow suicide. Death from lung cancer, death from heart disease, death from atherosclerosis. No matter what rationalization you come up with, smoking very definitely can, and most likely will, kill you.

Do's

In order for all the cells to perform their functions efficiently, our bodies need six basic groups of nutrients: (1) water; (2) vitamins; (3) minerals; (4) carbohydrates; (5) proteins; (6) fats. The proper combination of these six—as well as the elimination of sugar, caffeine, excess salt, excess alcohol, excess cholesterol, excess fat and drugs—will result in a healthy daily diet. Combine this healthy diet with Basic Training and your heart will beat stronger, your blood will flow more easily through its vessels because of your lowered blood pressure, and the chances of atherosclerosis and its attendant heart problems will diminish dramatically. Again, the following discussion of the six necessary nutrients is meant simply as an introductory guide.

Water

Water is the major component of the body. It transports chemicals throughout the body and acts as the medium in which most cellular use and storage of other nutrients takes place. The Basic Training athlete should drink at least eight 8-ounce glasses of water or water-based liquids (like fruit juices) a day.

Vitamins

If you eat a good, balanced diet of unrefined food, you should receive all the vitamins you need. A serious deficiency in a certain vitamin will result in a severe malnutrition problem—severe vitamin D deficiency results in rickets, for example. A minor deficiency in several of the less vital vitamins, more likely the case in the United States, can cause sub-

clinical malnutrition problems such as frequent colds, or chronic fatigue, or less noticeable inefficiencies in your internal system. I take supplements of A, most of the B's, C, D, E, lecithin and folic acid. I feel that today's packaged foods cannot give me everything I need and I can't always get fresh foods. Be careful not to overdo vitamin supplements, however.

Minerals

Basically, minerals dictate how much water your body can hold and where it is stored. Minerals also control muscle contractions and heartbeat and are necessary for the conduction of nerve impulses. Although you need thirteen different minerals, five are most essential: potassium, magnesium, sodium, calcium and iron. Minerals come from the soil, so your most direct access to them in the food chain is through those things that grow directly from the soil: vegetables, fruits, nuts and grains.

Fruits, particularly bananas, as well as vegetables, soy beans, wheat germ, rye flour, walnuts, pecans and molasses, contain potassium, the mineral that controls nerve conduction and muscle heat. Potassium deficiency is quite common among athletes and exercisers. Strenuous activity causes muscles to heat, so to cool themselves down the muscles release potassium into the bloodstream to carry heat away from the muscle. Once that job is done, the potassium is excreted in sweat and urine. That is why people who have diarrhea or older people who take diuretics have to watch out for potassium deficiency, the symptoms of which include weakness, irritability and overall fatigue.

Magnesium helps to control muscle contractions and to regulate the conversion of carbohydrates into energy. Like potassium, magnesium is lost through sweat and excretion. So you need to replenish it by eating leafy green vegetables, nuts, dark bread and by avoiding other alcoholic beverages in favor of beer.

Magnesium deficiency reveals itself in about the same way that low levels of potassium do: You feel weak and tired in general and over a long period of time. Nutritionists call this the "mineral blues." Too little magnesium can also up the frequency of muscle cramps. On the other hand, athletes who have lots of magnesium in their bodies may have frequent and massive bowel movements. Scientists theorize that the body releases large amounts of its magnesium into the intestinal tract during vigorous activity. (The common household cathartic called Epsom salts is really just magnesium sulfate.)

We need calcium for bone building and other cellular functions—no matter how old we are. The problem is that most people eat far too much beef, and though beef contains calcium, it does not contain vitamin D. Vitamin D must be present in the body before calcium can be absorbed. In other words, dairy products (such as milk, yogurt and cheese) with their attendant vitamin D offer the best source of usable calcium.

Anemia, or iron deficiency, can be a problem. Iron is vital to transporting oxygen in the blood, and some women may want to take regular iron supplements. Unfortunately, most foods extremely rich in iron are also extremely rich in cholesterol—liver, egg yolk and shellfish.

All the negatives of sodium (salt) and its relation to high blood pressure were discussed under "Don'ts." But remember that *some* salt is needed in the body for water control: One-fifth of one gram daily is plenty.

The body definitely needs other minerals such as phosphorus, fluorine, cobalt and zinc. Do some reading on minerals at the same time as you are studying vitamins. Also, you can buy mineral tablets separately from vitamins if you wish.

Carbohydrates

If you're looking for a pregame meal or an energy booster for exercise, you've found it. Donna deVarona, multi–gold-medal winner in the 1964 Olympics and now a television commentator, was an athlete ahead of her time. While all her swimming teammates sat down to the steak training table the day before competition, Donna filled herself up with spaghetti, a rich source of carbohydrates. Carbohydrates constitute the athlete's and the exer-

ciser's primary source of energy for robust physical activity.

Starches, like unrefined bread, potatoes and pasta, require only a few steps before they can be broken down into glucose and stored as energy; therefore, they comprise efficient sources of the fuel your muscles need to work hard and long. They do not jolt your adrenal system like simple sugars.

An even better source of carbohydrates than starches are raw or lightly cooked fruits and vegetables, eaten with their skins (and fruit and vegetable juices). Not only will they provide the same efficient energy source, they will also furnish several important vitamins and minerals.

I shoot for 50 percent of my daily calories in the form of complex carbohydrates. If you are active (and as a Basic Training athlete you are), you will use this energy source daily without storing excess fat.

Proteins

We already know that too many animal protein foods means too much cholesterol and fat. Protein accounts for about 40 percent of my daily calories—high enough to provide essential amino acids. If you tend to get your proteins from dairy products, make sure to drink low-fat milk and eat low-fat yogurt. You don't need the excess fats; the low-fat varieties have all the protein, vitamin D, calcium and other things you need.

Contrary to the steak-before-the-big-game myth, protein is never a source of immediate energy for sports or exercise. We do need protein because it is the primary material of which cells and tissues are built. But we needn't eat meat to get it, since legumes (beans, peas, etc.) and nuts, grains and dairy products offer plenty. Protein contains 23 different amino acids, 14 of which the body manufactures, and 9 of which we need to get from food. A combination of corn (with 7) and beans (with 2) can provide the 9 essential amino acids. Red meat contains all 9, but it also contains too much fat and cholesterol. I prefer fish or chicken.

Also contrary to training-table legend, protein requirements do not increase with exercise. The body has no place to store extra protein, so what you don't use, you store as glycogen and/or fat. In addition, the *fat* in the meat is *also* stored. Steak or any meat or food with a high-fat content is a lousy preexercise meal. Not only does it not provide immediate energy needed for the upcoming exercise, but it also takes a long time to digest and therefore can take away energy from the athlete's working muscles and heart by routing part of the oxygen-carrying blood supply to the also working digestive system.

Fats

Carbohydrates provide the primary source of muscle energy during exercise, but fat provides the muscles their primary source of energy at rest. Fat is burned as fuel by the muscles when the muscles have been depleted of glycogen, so the more you use your muscles through exercise, the less fat you'll carry around as dead weight—depending, of course, upon how much fat you eat. You should shoot for no more than 10 percent of your daily calories in fat. Less than 10 percent is preferable.

Stored as a secondary source of energy for endurance athletes, fat has its value. But in regular athletes, Basic Training athletes and inactive people, a too-high body-fat percentage is an extra load that makes the heart and muscles work harder to perform the same amount of activity that a leaner person could perform with less expenditure of effort.

If you can slip under 20 percent body-fat percentage, as a woman, you are heading in the right direction—under 18 percent is ideal. But just remember that approximately 10 percent of your total body weight, as a woman, is all the fat you need to protect the delicate organs, to help in the production of bile, to insulate the body slightly and to provide a medium for fat-soluble vitamins. All the fat over 10 percent of your total body weight is, cruel as it sounds, excess blubber.

As a general rule, your body will tell you what it needs to eat if you let it. By "let it," I mean forego excessive amounts of the items under "Don'ts" and eat sensible proportions of the "Do's," and see what happens over time. My guess is that, if you're at all like me, you will develop a taste for the foods that are good for you, and eating will become even more enjoyable than it is now.

EPILOGUE

I emphasize to you that the process of developing my physical potential has been a worthy enterprise for me—as a human being, not simply as a professional athlete. I have written every sentence of this book with the genuine hope that you will discover the development of your own physical potential to be equally worthy. It moves me to think that you will gain in strength, self-reliance, self-assurance. It is exciting to me that you will soon link your new powerful and efficient body with a new outlook on the quality of your life—more energy, more confidence, more ambition!

Physical training itself is not a panacea for everything, but through it you can build yourself a granite foundation of fitness that can enhance everything you do. The body may not be a temple, but it *is* a gift—the gift of movement that is your access to experience. When I am in shape, I am so proud and that pride shows in my career, my relationships, my everyday encounters. You already have all the resources you need to get in shape; and now you have a step-by-step guide from your coach, who believes in you. Basic Training is the best way I know to develop these resources and I offer it to you, at once thrilled to imagine your forthcoming growth and discoveries and fearful that you might not be as serious over the long haul about taking charge of your life as I am about taking charge of mine. This program does not take up much time, but it *will* require discipline to incorporate it as a natural, unsacrificeable part of your life.

The decision to use what you have and what I've offered is entirely up to you. As we all know too well, the fulfillment of wishes doesn't just cascade down upon us from the sky—everyone must back up her hopes with effort. I am not the only one who has ever conceived of a lifetime as some kind of adventurous process of being in training. In a book called *Autumn Garden*, Lillian Hellman reports this portion of a speech by writer Dashiell Hammett:

That big hour of decision, the turning point in your life, the someday you've counted on when you'd suddenly wipe out your past mistakes, do the work you'd never done, think the way you'd never thought, have what you'd never had, it just doesn't come suddenly. You trained yourself for it while you waited—or you've let it all run past you and frittered yourself away.

Your physical potential is too valuable to the rest of your life to fritter it away. I urge you to join the Basic Training team.

INDEX

414
3